THE GIRL
ON THE
ESCALATOR

THE GIRL

ON THE

TIGHTROPE BOOKS

ESCALATOR

/ Jim Nason /

Tightrope Books
602 Markham Street
Toronto, Ontario
M6G 2L8 Canada
www.TightropeBooks.com

ONTARIO ARTS COUNCIL
CONSEIL DES ARTS DE L'ONTARIO

Canada Council   Conseil des Arts
for the Arts   du Canada

Edited by Shirarose Wilensky.
Copyedited by John Greenwell & Alanna Lipson.
Cover design by David Bigham.
Typesetting by Shirarose Wilensky.
Cover art is *Escalator* by Chris Pelletiere.
Author photo by David Leyes.

Produced with the support of the Canada Council for the Arts and the Ontario Arts Council.

Printed in Canada on 100% post-consumer recycled paper.

LIBRARY AND ARCHIVES CANADA CATALOGUING IN PUBLICATION

Nason, Jim, 1957–
    The girl on the escalator / Jim Nason.

Short stories.
ISBN 978-1-926639-35-2

    I. Title.

PS8577.A74G57 2011   C813'.54   C2010-907364-9

For V.J.

CONTENTS

/ BRACES /

liked being an only child. Other kids at school had to share their toys and their bedrooms. Some of them even had to wear their older sibling's hand-me-downs. Not me. Two pink walls, two blue walls—I had a room all for myself. "Mine. Mine. It's all mine," I would say to the television screen after a marathon morning of Batman and Robin. Life in east end Montreal for a twelve-year-old kid like me was pretty good in 1968. There was only one small problem: My mother wanted a girl and my father wanted a boy. How could I be both?

"Hey Dad, let's take in an Expos game tomorrow." I tried imitating one of his buddies from the glass factory on Dorchester and Eighteenth when he walked into the room and turned off the television.

"Your mother wants you in the kitchen," is all he said.

Dad makes such lovely lanterns, I'd say to my mother. Of course I didn't say this out loud, it was just in my head, because the rule was no talking while baking. *The one he brought home is absolutely stunning*, I imagined saying, not allowing the effect to go too over-the-top, as I stirred the cookie dough, added droplets of water.

Well, okay, there was one other problem—the issue of my crooked legs. I had to wear these braces with clamps and screws and stuff. My father hated the noise, said that I "walk like a girl. All that swishing, side-to-side, from the hips."

"He's right," my mother said, sifting flour into the mix. "Not very boy-like."

Excuse me, I'd think, *there's a kid in this nuts-and-bolts-*

body. Where's the empathy? Where's the encouragement and support? Where's a good sibling when you need an ally most?

I talked too much, was the other complaint. They both hated that, so I tried not to talk at all. I wouldn't say a thing all day, except to the mirror: "Mine. Mine. It's all mine." I didn't say goodbye when my father kissed me on top of the head as he picked up his lunch bag and keys off the kitchen table. I didn't say, "Yes, Mother," when she asked if I had taken my vitamin D. I just nodded my head up and down, and got a good slap for not answering properly, sugar and flour flying all over the dusty-rose table. "What in heaven's name is wrong with you?" she asked. My mother was on to me. No normal twelve-year-old boy bakes cookies with his mother and insists on wearing the darted-with-red-tulips apron. Even though I tried to make it look like a blacksmith's dirty apron by folding it in two (I did leave the flower side out) and rubbing baker's chocolate all over it, my obsessive need to have clean fingernails was too telling. I licked them off dainty-like, the way I saw Eva Gabor do on *Green Acres*.

"Do any of the other boys stay inside all day with their mothers?" she asked. *Why does she ask me a gazillion questions if she wants me to stop talking so much? Why does she ask me questions that are too delicious to answer without stirring up trouble?* "Of course they do," I said, slowly adding more water to the mix. "Only none of them get the privilege of going to visit the doctor three times a week with her as well."

"Go to your room," she said. "Now."

I untied the apron slowly, folded it in four, dropped it on the floor.

"Pick-that-thing-up," she said. "Move it!"

I pushed myself off the yellow vinyl chair. I went *clink clink clink* across the kitchen floor with my head down, step-by-step up to my two-pink-walls, two-blue-walls bedroom, with my very own television. All in all, life was good as an only child. I lined up G.I. Joe, Ken, and Barbie, put them face down on the pillow.

"And no playing with dolls," she yelled from the bottom of the stairs.

Dolls weren't really her big worry at the moment. I could hear her on the princess phone, trying to dial slowly. As if she could control the speed of the dial. As if she could control who answered—Doctor Raisin Eyes or his receptionist.

Later at the dinner table, I continued my silence. Legs sticking out like a giant metal slingshot, I sat up straight with my shoulders back and looked at my dad with reassuring masculine agreement when he read out loud from the Business section of the *Gazette*; and I smiled at my mother tenderly when she mentioned that she had heard that Morag and Frank O'Neil were getting a divorce. But I didn't open my mouth except to push in a meatball or noodle. At times, though, I thought that I would burst: "ATSCHOOLTO-DAYONEOFTHEKIDSHITANOTHERKIDANDTHETEACHER-HITTHEKIDWITHAYARDSTICKNANDHEPEEDHISPANTS . . ." Sometimes I couldn't help myself and the words just shot out of my mouth like water from a hole in a busted dam.

"A little peace and quiet at the dinner table would be nice," my father said.

"Did he really pee his pants?" my mother asked.

/ / /

"TIGHTEN THE SCREWS," the doctor said. "Got to tighten the screws or the boy will look like a giant *O* by time he's a twelve," he said to my mother, who got her hair coloured and Beehived on the way to the doctor's office, and put on high heels in the waiting room. His accent was hard to understand sometimes—it wasn't French, maybe Italian? He always had a tan and his shiny brown eyes looked like chocolate-covered raisins.

"I'm twelve already," I said, and was sure that I saw him put his hand up her skirt when she leaned forward, pretending to want to hear what I said.

"Here's a colouring book," said Doctor Raisin Eyes.

"Colouring is for little kids," I said.

"Take this then," he said, grabbing a magazine off his desk. "Wait outside. And milk from now on. No more Pepsi-Cola."

The Journal of Family Physicians got my attention. A giant orange boob like a grapefruit or melon, only with scars. *Peau d'orange—Advanced Breast Cancer*. And the heart. A picture of a real bloody heart in some live guy's chest. *Doctor Christian Barnard—Film Star Surgeon does it again!* Then there was the foot. It was all pink and black, full of pus, and one of the toes was missing.

"What's taking so long?" I cried out.

"I'll go see," said the receptionist. "I'd be happy to." She smiled, flung open the door to the examining room without knocking.

/ / /

"DON'T YOU DARE say a word to your father," my mother said later, as I *clink clinked* down the sidewalk behind her, not believing what I saw earlier. *Brother or sister. Where the hell is a good sibling witness when you need one?* I asked myself, the words budding and busting in my Ken-doll, Barbie-doll head.

The next visit, I asked for *The Journal of Family Physicians* right away.

"No problem," said Doctor Raisin Eyes. My mother had already put the *Do Not Disturb* sign on the door.

"I like the pictures," I said to the receptionist, who was on the telephone.

"She's here now," she whispered to the person on the other end. And I knew that she was talking about my mother.

/ / /

"PATRICK," MY MOTHER said a few months later, "you're getting a little brother or sister." My parents had sat me down between them on the living room sofa. "Your leg braces are coming off and I'm going to have a little one," my mother said, patting her stomach. My father pretended to smile, but I saw the question mark in his eyes when he looked across to her as she lowered her head, sipped her tea

"Mine. Mine. Mine. She's all mine," I said in my bedroom later. I'll dress her in pink frills and brush her hair. I'll teach him how to throw a ball and chase the girls. *Mine. Mine. Mine. He's all mine.* But there's no way I'm sharing this room. And he can have Mom, but I'm keeping Dad. No. The new kid can have him and I'll keep her. I need Mom to help me destroy Doctor Raisin Eyes. It's my duty to the world, my responsibility as Batman to crusade against the forces of evil.

/ / /

"TIGHTEN THE SCREWS," he says. "Got to tighten the screws or the boy will be like a giant *O* by the time he's a twelve." My mother got her hair coloured and Beehived on the way, only now she can't bend over to put on the high heels in the waiting room where he makes her wait.

"I'm twelve already," I say.

"You are big boy now," says Doctor Raisin Eyes. "Big boy," he says, putting his cold stethoscope against my heaving chest. "And your mama tells me you have imagination like giant."

"MYMOM'SBRAINISMISSINGAFEWCELLS," I say, my inside voice jumping out.

/ / /

BROWN IS A boy's colour. Pink isn't. One day my mother buys

me a chocolate brown shirt with ice cream pink stripes. "Your father will be fine with this," she says. "It's okay if the pink is mixed in. Quick. Put it on before he gets home."

Yelling. My father yelling and crying. My mother crying and yelling back. Then there is quiet and me under my one blue blanket and one pink blanket wondering what I will do if my father comes into the room and asks about Doctor Raisin Eyes. "Hey, Dad, have you ever seen an orange boob?" I could ask him. But then I hear the hockey game: *He shoots! He scores!* and my father saying, "Yes! Yes!" That's a happy ending story. "Yes! Yes," he says when the Canadiens score, and I slowly leave the bed. The *clink clink clink* is muffled by the blanket I use to slide across the floor to open the door just a little—enough to let some light in, blue light from the television. Then I go to sleep, only I keep one eye open.

/ / /

THERE'S MORE. THERE'S the gross stuff like how the apartment stinks after my mother moves out. My father's stinkin' shoes and my father's stinkin' socks. "You're going to get gangrene," I want to tell him, but don't dare. Then there's his stinkin' Export 'A' cigarettes. The green kitchen walls stink and the brown carpet stinks in the living room where he picks his toenails with a screwdriver. The cat claws at the legs of the stinkin' chair and the spaghetti in the cold water stinks. *It feels like guts,* I tell myself. *That's what cold noodles feel like in the bottom of the burnt to nothin' pot.*

/ / /

"PEARLS?" MY FATHER asks.

"Yeah," I say. "What are pearls made of?"

"Oysters."

"Oysters?"

"Yeah," he says. "They come from oysters. Now take that necklace off your neck right now."

He was referring to my candy necklace. And before I can get a word out, he says, "Don't ask why. Just do it."

"But they're funner to eat when they're on your neck. Besides," I say, "they look nice."

I knew I'd crossed the line.

/ / /

I LOVE BEING the only child. Two blue walls, and another two blue walls. I get to spend an hour or so alone in my bedroom before my father comes in.

"No more sissy colours for you," he says, touching the wall to see if the paint has dried. Blue over the pink makes the walls look grey.

"And now that those braces are off, don't you think you could stop that swishing?" he tells me, swatting the back of my head. I look at my G.I. Joe for inspiration and am about to open my mouth, but he says, "Enough. Just go downstairs and clean up the mess in the kitchen."

The bubbles are my favourite part. Filling the sink until

it's almost overflowing and watching the pink and green Tupperware float in the suds. It's not so bad. Besides, one day I'm going to be a surgeon. I'm going to take people's hearts out and put them back in better, but only if they're nice. For now, it's bubbles, and my father yelling: "Hey Patrick, will you grab me a Pepsi from the fridge? Son, where does your mother keep the scissors?"

He talks like that. As if she's just gone to the hairdresser and will be right back.

"Patrick, what did she take out of the freezer for dinner?"

"I'll take out the hamburger," I answer, but he's not listening.

"Probably spaghetti again," he sighs. "She always makes spaghetti on Wednesday because it's two days before payday and it's got to last."

"I'll make spaghetti, Dad," I yell back, spinning the soapy Tupperware bowl on my finger.

"Leave those dishes for your mother," he says. "Get in here and shoot the shit with your dad," he says.

I love being an only kid. The next day, after my father goes to work, I find where my mother left the doilies, the plastic red roses, and a small white vase. I wipe off the coffee table with the dishcloth and make a nice arrangement of the ashtray and the flowers. My mother took the vacuum cleaner. She took the good dishes, too, and the little sister. I'm technically still an only child, that kid never spent a single night inside this house.

"It's a girl," she whispered into the phone. "You have a baby sister."

"Why are you whispering, Mom?" I asked. "He's not home."

"Well, I'm in the hospital, darling," she said. "And there's another mom in the next bed trying to rest."

"Well, I can hardly hear you," I told her. "Go use the phone in the hall or something."

"I can't," she said. "Mommy needs to rest for a while.

That was the last time I heard from her. Just like that, I got to be an only child again.

"You act like the mother," is what the kids tell me at school. "You wash the dishes like a girl, and you cook supper."

"I suppose you wash his friggin' dick too," says Michael Veecock.

"You *are* a dick," I say back. "Who has a name like VeeCOCK anyhow?" I say, and get dragged by my ear down to the principal's office.

"You're suspended," the principal says and gives me a note to give my father.

/ / /

"WHAT'S THIS?" HE asks.

I shrug my shoulders and he throws it onto the table near the ashtray, still folded in half, with CONFIDENTIAL scribbled on the front by the principal. So now I get to stay home and watch television during the day; I especially like the go-go girls dancing in white miniskirts. I pretend I'm Petula Clark and sing "Downtown" with her when she comes on.

When will that man get home? I sigh. *Supper is getting cold.* But sometimes he doesn't bother and I have to eat alone. I kind of miss the kids at school and I wish my father would call the principal, even if it means I'm going to be in trouble, because it beats being alone all day. "Hello out there," I say to the grey walls and the blue walls. "Is there anybody there?" I *clunk clunk clunk* across the living room in my father's paint-splattered slippers. I sit in front of the television, cross my almost straight legs, the way I imagine Eva Gabor would. *Mine. Mine. Mine. It's all mine,* I say inside my head.

/ NIBBLE /

t's a fact of nature: the brighter the light, the longer the shadow, and Amanda's hit the floor like a good seven feet of worry that morning. The sun was shining on the snow in the backyard and she was close enough to the kitchen window to see eggshells, coffee grinds, and other undescribables that the raccoons had scattered all the way over to the off-the-hinge gate. There were two slices of lemon pie left over from the night before—a big slice and an even bigger slice with just the tip nibbled off. Amanda was only half listening to Allan, her eyes squinting at the snow. Then the sun went behind a cloud and took the light from the kitchen and her shadow along with it.

"Mandy, that was a pretty sick joke—if you could call it a joke!"

"Amanda. Not Mandy," she said. "The *A* means something."

She put on her boots and coat, told Allan to let himself out, to put the door key under the trash can in the backyard. It was his first overnight at her place, but she knew where she could find him if he decided to walk away with the stereo or something.

She took the subway from Chester toward the Lee-Chin Crystal at the ROM, thinking about the whole pie and mouse thing. *How could I be so nasty to such a decent guy?* she wondered, but didn't dwell on it too long.

On the train, a boy sat across from her. Twenty below zero and he was wearing a thin white hoodie, black baggy jeans, and white sneakers with the laces undone. But the hoodie was what struck her. Well, not really the hoodie—other than looking really flimsy and clean it wasn't so unusual. It was the way the kid kept looking out but trying to hide his face at the same time. He was fidgeting with the lip of the hood, pulling it down over his eyes, looking up to the ceiling like a crackhead Lady Gaga. Only he was sickly pale and softer looking. He had a beauty mark under his big-bone nose. Despite the freezing subway car, there wasn't a shiver from that boy. That's what she really admired about him.

/ / /

AMANDA STANDS IN front of the ROM Crystal. Her purse is heavy with listings and the two books that she's reading. She's like that, she wants it all—to be the top real estate agent in the city who also finds time to read all the bestsellers. All the science fiction and romantic fantasy. All those enormous coffee table books on Frank Lloyd Wright and every twelve-step book she can wrap her fingers around. Some of them have even helped a little.

Amanda thinks of Allan. His quiet man's mouth, small as a Cheerio. Honestly, it's the teensiest, roundest mouth she's ever seen. Weird. Even weirder on a man as tall and handsome as Allan. Not tall and handsome like a movie star, but tall and handsome nonetheless. His curly blond hair hangs in front of his bluish eyes. He's not boyish, but a youthful looking thirty-five, and built like a slightly overweight basketball player. And pasted in the center of that face is that quiet-man, small-circle mouth. You can tell a lot by a person's mouth. Take

Anna Nicole Smith. Amanda figures that woman could never have been Marilyn, no matter how hard she tried—too much gum showing, too many teeth, too much white-trash damage in those bloodshot eyes.

/ / /

HER FATHER WAS a loud-mouth man, shouting out orders to his seven children. Except when he was drinking—then he was mostly sad and frowned lots. Amanda eventually figured out when a frown stands on its head, it becomes a smile. The only girl, she was the fat child with the brains.

"Do those handstand push-ups," she'd ask her father, because she knew he liked to show off his sergeant's muscles. She stood there with silver braces on her teeth and her roly-poly clown-girl mouth. She wore her plaid skirt with suspenders and black patent shoes. She laughed and cheered for him while he pressed up and down.

But that was a long time ago. No point in splitting your gut in the rewind comedy of childhood.

Focus, she tells herself. *You need to focus, Amanda.*

/ / /

ONCE, AFTER SOCIAL time, Allan asked her if she was drawn to their church because of the great shopping on Bloor. "Desire will kill you," he said in his quiet-man voice. "You should pray on your obsession."

Amanda was aware of the other parishioners pretending not to listen as they hovered close with Styrofoam cups of coffee, but she wanted to see where he was going. "No, Allan," she said. "I'm not here for the shopping."

According to her shrink, social rituals are good. He says she needs to connect with people. This socially progressive Anglican church came highly recommended. Amanda figured, what the hell, it couldn't hurt.

/ / /

THE FIRST TIME she saw a live mouse was in Cobourg, Ontario, on the army base. The houses were called PMQs—private married quarters—and it was Christmas. There had been a blizzard and the street was buried in snow. Nineteen-fifties postwar bungalows stood in a row with identical pristine front lawns—except theirs. There was a foil-wrapped present sticking out of the snow like the tip of a silver iceberg with a red ribbon.

"Take this," her mother slurred as she tossed his silver-foil Christmas present into the snow in the front yard. Amanda's father watched and laughed. They lived at 444 Burnett drive back then. The address was drilled into Amanda's brain each morning before she hopped onto the yellow school bus with the driver who wouldn't let girls sing songs with swear words in them. Four, plus four, plus four, added up to twelve—her father's favourite number.

The lit-up tree in the living room had tons of red and

green ornaments because her mother loved them. And tons and tons of silver tinsel because her father wanted to hang each strand one by one. Amanda could smell cigarette smoke on her new flannel nightie, and on the presents under the tree. Every Christmas Eve she was given a nightie, and her brothers got new pajamas with cowboys and Indians on them. That year there were six hockey sticks in a row—one for each of the boys—and a long box that she knew was a ready-to-assemble dollhouse from peeking at it when it was under her father's side of the bed. Her father was fixated on houses—probably had to do with the city-to-city and army-base-to-army-base moving thing.

/ / /

SHE REMEMBERS WAKING up to the grey sock, long and heavy, next to her in bed. It held a tiny plastic pony and a wind-up tin rabbit. There was also an orange and an apple, a pink comb and a pink brush, two pieces of fudge wrapped in wax paper, and a curvy piece of ribbon candy that was just thrown in so it stuck to the wool.

Her frown-mouth father sat on her bed blowing smoke at the ceiling. "Mandy, it's hard being a sergeant, ya know," he slurred into her ear. His whiskers felt rough, like a cat's tongue. "I even got shot once. In Korea," he said, rolling up his pant leg to show her his ugly white calf muscle, white as a peeled potato. "There's shrapnel under the skin. Feel," he said, placing her hand on the lump.

"You're twelve now," he said. "A big girl."

Amanda's throat was scratchy. "What's shrapnel?" she asked.

"Stay put," he said when she pulled back the covers to get out of bed.

The weight of him. The smell of him. The way she felt split in half. Amanda couldn't breathe and she couldn't move. She disappeared into a small black ball. Small as a chestnut. Then, she became smaller than a raisin. And finally, she was a black dot, like the tip of a crayon—floating above her bed, disappearing into the dark.

After he left, Amanda reached into the grey sock and found something that wasn't there before—a mirrored pendant.

She went down to the living room and curled up next to the presents under the lit-up tree, all with the same label: TO A, LOVE SANTA. Like her father's, all of the children's names begin with the letter A—Amanda, Adam, Alex, Andrew, Alvin, Abe, and Anthony.

Although the gifts were all marked with the same letter, he knew the contents of every package by where it was placed. He warned the children that the presents were like landmines and if you moved one, it would explode. Her mother, Beth, didn't have an A name. "Your mother's a B . . . ," her father would say, laughing, . . . "a real B."

That's when she saw the mouse. It was chewing its way into one of the boxes under the tree. Amanda thought she would explode. She squeezed her hand tightly around the shiny silver necklace. She closed her eyes and held her breath.

AT DINNER HER mother pours gravy. Her hands shaking over the turkey: "Amanda needs to stop crying at the dinner table," she says. "Stop fidgeting," she says to Adam. "Eat your peas, Alex." "Wipe your mouth," she tells Andrew. "Alvin and Abe, sit up straight." And "What's so funny?" she asks Anthony. Everyone knew Adam had his pet mouse hidden in his shirt. Anthony was in on the joke. They were all in on the joke. Except Beth.

/ / /

AMANDA AND ALLAN had an agreement—they would take things slow and just be friends. "After a year," she'd promised, "we'll reassess."

Allan knew about her father, and he understood about anorexia. He could be patient. Besides, his first marriage hadn't ended too well. He was in no hurry to rush into anything new. But mouse droppings in his pie? That was pure insanity. He would follow her and insist that she explain herself.

He locked the door to her house and put the key under the trash can as instructed. He drove to the Lee-Chin Crystal where he knew he'd find her.

He paced and paused, stood and watched from a distance. She looked weighted down, bent over. She was shivering. He stood beside her. "Mandy," he said. "You're freezing."

She didn't answer. She looked up into the glass above her.

Together, they were stretched and blurred.

"I knew you'd show up here, Allan," she said. "It's no accident you have the same name as my father."

/ / /

IT WAS HIS idea to eat the pie for breakfast. "What the heck," he'd said. "Besides, you're thin as a rake."

"What's with this 'thin-as-a-rake' nonsense?" she'd asked, gulping back a caffeine pill with her coffee.

They were sitting in front of the patio doors off the kitchen. Amanda looked out at the snow, trying to avoid his watery blue eyes. She'd wanted to clean up the mess the raccoons had made in the yard, screw the gate back on its hinges, anything to get the day moving. But he didn't seem to be in a hurry to leave.

"So . . ." she said, handing him a fork. "Celine Dion walks into a Vegas bar . . ."

"Is nothing sacred to you, Mandy?"

"What are you talking about, Allan? It's a Celine Dion joke, not a Mother Teresa joke, for crying out loud!"

"Why would you want to pick on Celine Dion?"

"Do you want to hear the joke or not?"

"Well, okay. As long as it's not another one about how she married her father."

"She didn't marry her father," Amanda said.

"Might just as well have. She was only twelve when René hit on her. Just tell the joke. Please."

"Too late."

"What do you mean, 'too late'?"

"Timing," she said. "You've ruined it. Timing's everything in a joke."

Then he put his hand on her knee. "Take an inventory of everything you buy for twelve weeks," Allan said, nibbling her ear. "Do you know how beautiful you are?"

She thought she'd vomit. "Twelve?" she asked. "Why twelve weeks?"

"It's a random number. You've talked about wanting to deal with your shopping obsession at church."

She gave him the slice of pie with the tip missing, the mouse dropping like a half-worm buried inside.

/ / /

ONE TIME SHE was in the subway, standing on the damp platform in some poster-splattered station. Lost. Watching mice the same silver colour as the dust-covered rails running in and out of a hole in the wall, she was trying to make sense of the subway map and feeling cranky because she wanted to get to the good shopping in Yorkville, but the train just wouldn't come. She studied the map. *You Are Here.* She put her finger on the dot and arrow. Then she noticed a beggar a little way down the platform. He was a dwarf with no arms. And he looked poor and miserable, like a character straight out of *La Bohème*. She walked closer to him and could see he had a tattoo with writing on the crown of his stump. He smiled, so she walked closer, trying to read his tattoo: YOU ARE HERE, with an arrow and a dot. The gods of synchronicity were with her and she knew the train would arrive any minute. She dropped five dollars in his hat and walked away feeling strangely content.

/ / /

THE SNOW IN the backyard had turned to ice. The sun came through the window like a spotlight shining directly down on Allan's slice of lemon pie.

"What's this?" he yelled, falling off his chair, his small-circle, quiet-man mouth becoming enormous, spitting out pie, pointing with his extra long middle finger at Amanda.

She wasn't going to let him make a big deal about it. As Allan got up off the floor, she started clearing the dishes from the table. "So Celine Dion walks into a bar . . ." she said over her shoulder, ". . . and the bartender . . ."

"Okay. I've just eaten what looks like a mouse turd and you want to finish your stupid joke routine."

"Stupid? You haven't even heard the joke yet."

"So go ahead then," he'd said. "I'm sure it's more important than the insanity of this pie thing."

"No. You've ruined it."

"Well, start over then."

"Celine Dion walks into a bar and the bartender says: 'So Celine, why the long face?' " Amanda cracked up. And when she could see that Allan's quiet-man mouth had reverted to a small *O*, she stopped laughing.

"I don't get it," he said.

/ / /

THE NIGHT BEFORE, Allan had yelled from the bathroom: "There's no mirror in here!"

"It's in the linen closet," she'd yelled back.

A few minutes later, he came into the bedroom. She was already under the covers, in the dark. He crawled under the sheets. It had been a year. "I'm ready," she'd said. His feet were cold and his breath smelled like mint. He reached across her and turned on the bedside lamp. "You are so incredibly thin, Mandy," he'd said, running his fingers down her side. "I can count every-single-one-of-these-ribs."

When she started to get out of the bed, he pulled her toward him and began nibbling on her ear. "But you're still sexy," he'd said.

Penis sizes fascinate her. She has had sex with four men—a variety of widths and lengths—the penises, that is. Frank, in grade ten, was short and skinny; his penis was long and fat. John, from the real estate course, was overweight and tall—his was short and fat as a mushroom. Allan is tall and thin, she thought that maybe his penis would be proportionate. She is wrong. She takes it in her hand and is startled by its diminutive size. Stiff and tiny, like a bullet or crayon, it doesn't seem to grow, even when he is inside her. She is relieved and disappointed.

A few minutes later, at the instant of his climax, a mouse ran across her pillow like a brilliant idea.

"Where are you going?" he'd asked.

"There was a mouse on my pillow."

"There's no mouse, Mandy," he'd said.

"Amanda, not Mandy," she'd whispered and tiptoed toward the kitchen and the two slices of pie they had left on the table because he was in a big rush to get to the bedroom.

/ / /

SO HIS APPEARANCE at the Lee-Chin doesn't surprise her.

"There are nice guys in this world, Amanda," he says, kicking at the snow. "Even guys with the same name as your father."

He had asked Father Doug: "How can I change all that bad history in her?"

"It's not your place, Allan," he'd said. "Leave that girl, and her past, alone."

/ / /

AMANDA FIGURES THERE are no accidents. Take the other day, for instance. She was walking up from Osgoode subway and she'd passed two women selling black buttons with roses on them to mark the anniversary of the Montreal Massacre. She had bought a button and was thinking of all those murdered women. For some bizarre reason, Annie Lennox's song "Why" popped into her head. That sad and melancholy song played over and over inside her head. She was humming "Why" as she walked up the exit stairs from the subway. As she got to the top step, right there, on University Avenue, there was a *Toronto Sun* mailbox and the headline, in big bold letters: **WHY?** The story was about a woman who jumped off a bridge after throwing her baby first. The child survived, but they figured she was damaged for good.

/ / /

EACH BAG CONTAINED a pair of gloves, a hat, a scarf, a toothbrush, toothpaste, a comb, a mirror, a pair of wool socks, and a chocolate bar.

"Why a mirror?" Allan asked.

"Because they get a comb," she said.

"Why a chocolate bar?" he asked.

"Because everyone deserves something good in her life," she said.

Every Sunday morning for almost a year, Allan would arrive at her small house in Riverdale with two empty boxes. She would be waiting at the door. She would never invite him inside. Together, on the front porch, they would load the gift bags into the boxes. Then they would carry them to his green Volkswagen parked by the curb.

"You're tall. Why would you buy such a small car?" she asked.

Allan seemed puzzled. He gave her question a good deal of

thought. They drove almost two blocks before he answered.

"I didn't buy it," he said. "My wife did."

"Your ex?"

"She died of breast cancer," he said, and drove another two blocks before speaking again.

"You know, it's very kind of you to bring these gifts to the Outreach program, Amanda," he said.

"Thank you," she said. She was sad about the wife.

/ / /

AMANDA LOOKS UP, marvels at the dramatic structure, the architect's vision, his whimsical brilliance. Mirrors. Glass. The extension like a luminous meteor lodged into the side of the original museum.

YOU ARE HERE: the map at the building entrance—*guidance or affirmation?* she wonders.

/ / /

WHEN SHE WAS very young, probably three or four, Amanda had a dream of green horses and pink rabbits.

"Of course green horses can fly, sweetheart," her father had said. "But who has ever heard of pink rabbits who can bark," he'd added, getting down on his hands and knees, barking and chasing her while she ran around the living room in search of a chair to climb up on, screeching and laughing, kicking at her father's pretend wild-rabbit bark.

STANDING UNDER THE Crystal is like standing in a circus fun-house—Amanda looks long and thin, or short and fat—depending where she's standing and how the light hits the mirrors and glass. And there's Allan. She knows that he is the personification of too much sun. She doesn't mean too much sun like Club Med. She's thinking about Doris Day too much sun. Too saccharine. All sunshine and lollipops is dangerous.

"Where's your dark side, Allan?" she asks, but he is already walking away into the standstill traffic on Bloor, with his sad-man shoulders bent, his shadow dragging behind him through the snow. "People who don't show their bad side make me nervous," she says.

"People who show their good side make you more nervous," he shouts back. "See you at church next week?"

Amanda doesn't answer. She looks up. She is here, and here, and here—up in a long strip of mirrored glass that repeats itself over and over.

So, Celine Dion walks into a bar and the bartender says . . .

Amanda kicks at the snow, clutches her coat to her throat.

Why the long face?

/ FLAME /

The streetcar driver is bearded and grumpy, but his voice is that of a pleasantly robotic young woman. He brakes and I fall forward, almost dropping the jewellery box tucked under my arm. "Excuse me," I say, but get a dirty look from the guy I crashed into, standing with his arms outstretched reading the paper, even though we're all sandwiched in so friggin' tight it's hard to breathe. *On chi my big meanie. On chi my big meanie*, pops into my head. I shift the black lacquered box with the ivory stars to my other arm; the box is small, but it's heavy.

"Gerrard. Gerrard Street, Don Jail, and Chinatown east," the pre-recorded musical voice announces as the grumpy driver slams on the brakes and everyone falls forward, including newspaper guy and his too-early-in-the-morning-for-it attitude. Most of the passengers get off and newspaper guy leaves his *Sun* on an empty seat—it's Super Tuesday and anything can happen. The Americans may get their first black President. They may get their first female President. Ice Lady, they call her. Big Business with Boobs. And even though I'm on a crowded streetcar on a snowy February day in Toronto, I find myself imagining Hillary and Bill starting their big day in Washington. They are seated at a surprisingly small table in a sunny room. They call it The Breakfast Room. It's painted yellow, like the sundresses that Chelsea probably wore as a child. There are flowers on the table, yellow or red tulips. The floor is retro looking with black-and-white tiles in a checkerboard pattern. It's clean and shiny, and there's plenty of light reflected off the snow through the

French doors that lead out onto the patio where Bill was sent to smoke. He stands and kisses Hillary goodbye. He has bad breath: cigar and egg. She brushes a few flakes of dandruff off his shoulders, takes a bite of her slightly burnt toast, goes back to reading the paper.

/ / /

MY FATHER'S NAME is Bill too. As far as he was concerned, cigars were for show-off idiots. His blue dress pants were always pressed perfect, his white shirts ironed with starch. We lived in Montreal back then. On the nights when my parents went dancing, he shaved twice because his whiskers were so heavy. These days, people would say that he looks like George Clooney. Back then, they said Montgomery Clift. She was like Lana Turner without the sexy sweaters. His black hair was slicked back with Brylcreem and he smelled like Aqua Velva. I don't remember the smell of Aqua Velva, I only know that the bottle is blue and that his ironed shirt smelled like sun and deodorant. He sat with his legs apart and held his head high when he laughed at the television. He clapped his hands, and sometimes left the living room and came back with two big spoons, shiny as the knives that we were glad he left in the kitchen drawer. We wanted to leave, but he made us stay—it was the worst show ever, *Don Messer's Jubilee*. My father watched and waited for the chance to hold his head high, tap his foot, and slap those sparkling spoons on his knee along with the fiddle, square dancers moving in and out, side by side, and me and my mother not saying a word.

Later, I couldn't sleep. I tossed and turned, kicked the blankets off, pulled them on again, remembering the way he teased her the day before—"On chi my big meanie," my father repeated over and over.

/ / /

I WONDER IF Monica hadn't said anything, how Hillary would have found out. I wonder if Monica still carries a little black purse with matches for cigars.

/ / /

I AM TEN years old. I come down here at least once a week. My father built this box for laundry because he wanted to show how he could use a hammer. It holds a lot of dirty clothes and it's pretty much full every time. Sometimes I eat whatever I've stolen from Dépanneur Black Cat—usually Juicy Fruit or licorice. Sometimes I sleep. I can't sleep at night, but I sleep during the day if I'm in the box. It's hard to climb in and get the lid closed, and it smells like pee and work socks. At first the blackness scares me, but then I get used to it and kind of get a tingly feeling inside and start to like the smell of wet towels and socks and stuff. The hard part is sitting still when my mother comes downstairs to wash his shirt in the sink.

"Go make your father something to eat," she'd said, after their fight. "Kraft Dinner."

I told her that I didn't know how, and she said, "Boil water. Add that orange powder."

But when I brought it to him he threw it against the living room wall. It splashed over everything—the curtains, the television, his white shirt.

She pulls the string for the light above the sink. Through a crack in the wood, I watch her turn on the water and start scrubbing with a brush. Then he is there, in his blue dress pants and no shirt, standing behind her.

"Aren't you my big meanie?" she says when he puts his arms around her waist and kisses her hair.

"What did you say?" he asks.

"He's just a little kid," she says. My father steps back. I pull a damp pillowcase over my head, squeeze down lower. "On chi my big meanie. On chi my big meanie," he mocks her. She doesn't cry or scream like she usually does. After, he opens the lid to the laundry box, throws his wet shirt inside. *On chi my big meanie*, I rhyme in my head, when he drags me by the arm out of the box and the light hurts my eyes.

/ / /

THE NEXT DAY my arm is sore and so are my legs.

"No point in dwelling on it," my mother says. "Now watch the door," she adds, as she digs around in my father's coat pocket. I hear jingling and decide to come back later and get the coins. We are at the closet by the front door, he's in the bathroom puking. I look at her bruised eye. It's not black or blue like the movies, it's yellow and green, spread out. I will find a way to beat him up when I am grown-up.

"Take this," she says, handing me the ripped off corner of a cigarette package with a number written in pink lipstick. "With God as my witness, I'll tear it to shreds and burn it."

/ / /

NOT TOO BIG, *not too small, just the size of Mon-tree-all,* I sing in my head. We are on the Côte-des-Neiges bus and this woman with a beard and a long grey coat that looks like a ratty old blanket with big buttons sits across the aisle from us. My mother says that it's not polite to stare, but I keep looking anyhow. "It's the lady from Expo," I tell her. From La Ronde.

"How come she doesn't shave it off?" I ask, all excited and loud enough for most of the people on the bus to hear.

"Shhh," my mother whispers, squeezes my hand. We are going to St. Joseph's Oratory. My mother has a white winter coat. There is a red suitcase at her feet and the black jewellery box with the ivory stars on the lid in her lap.

She says, "We are going to walk up every single one of those goddamn stairs."

"It's snowy," I say.

"Only angel's dandruff," she says.

The weird lady gets off the bus first. It's a long way up to the church with crutches and canes hanging over the walls, and Brother Andre's heart in a red box. People are working their way up the wooden steps—most of them are old women wearing heavy coats and black scarves covering their heads, some have rosaries in their hands with gloves that have no fingers. The lady with the beard is on her knees.

"I imagine she has plenty to pray about, and I told you to stop staring," my mother says, pushing me by the back of the head past the lady, who is crawling, step-by-step, up through the snow.

I turn back and look up at my mother, tell her, "Icicles are probably going to grow on those whiskers by the time that lady reaches the top."

She says, "Do you have to talk so friggin' much? They'll thaw out in heaven. Now get moving, young man."

"What's on the other side?" I ask.

"The cemetery."

"What's a cemetery?"

"Why are you such a chatterbox?"

"What's a cemetery?"

"It's for dead people."

"Oh," I say.

"Oh," she says back. "Up you go."

/ / /

IN THE CHURCH there are thousands of candles. We kneel in the front pew. I look up at the crucifix—the thorns on his head, his ribs sticking out, his legs crossed, the nails in his bloody feet.

"Don't stare at God," she says.

I tell her, "It's Jesus, not God."

"Don't correct me," she says and slaps me on the hand—right there, right in front of Jesus and Mary and all those statues of saints with purple light behind them standing in a circle around the church. I tell God, in my head, *I'm sorry about the dollar and twelve cents I stole from my father's coat pocket. Besides,* I explain, *he bought me two packs of baseball cards and sat in the chair by my bed reading when I couldn't fall asleep.*

After a few minutes I feel her elbow in my ribs, so we slide along the pew in the direction of the candles—hundreds and hundreds of them burning in rows.

"Do you have it?" she asks.

"I don't think this is what the candles are for," I say, but hand her the paper with the pink lipstick numbers on it, then I stand back. She throws it on the candles, opens the black jewellery box and takes out one torn-off paper, then another and another, throws them on the fire. We stand back and watch the flames.

"*Mardi spectacle!*" says the priest with a red fire extinguisher that's hardly big enough to put out a single match. "*Allons-y,*" he says to me and my mother, pointing to the giant doors at the back of the church.

Going downhill is easier. My mother is a few feet ahead of me, walking fast. Because of her white coat I don't see her fall at first. Then I see the black box and the red suitcase. *Why are you crying?* I want to ask, but don't. Instead, I touch the sleeve of her coat.

"Mommy will come back for you," she says, handing me the jewellery box. She stays on the ground, blends in with the snow. "Keep it," she says. "Now go back up there and help put that fire out."

/ / /

WHEN YOU THINK about it, I could have figured out how to find her long before my thirty-third birthday. I wanted to show her how well things turned out. I do work that I love, have lots of friends, and I'm happy most of the time. I wanted to tell her the old guy mellowed and seems genuinely sorry for being such a jerk.

It was simple. I went to the Toronto Reference Library and picked up the Montreal telephone book: she was in it. She'd called one night, drunk, when I was about eighteen and asked if *he* was around. When I said no, she told me that she got a job as a cook and that she was living with some guy named Jacques who spent most of his time in a wheelchair. "Now I'm the one who does the shoving around," she said, laughing into the telephone. She had a French accent and told me where she lived.

"You can come visit if you want," she said.

/ / /

I WAIT ALMOST fifteen years, then wrap the jewellery box in my grey sweater, place it in my gym bag along with my shaving kit, clean socks, and underwear. The drive in the rented car to Montreal is icy. Rain then snow, then ice-rain all the way. I count fourteen cars in the ditch, and then stop counting. The house is right off the highway, just like she said it would be. It's leaning to one side.

It's weird to hold her. She's heavier, and she's even shorter than I remembered. She kisses me on the lips, says she missed me. It's like kissing a strange woman and I feel funny about her breasts pressing up against me. Then, like an afterthought, she points to an old man in a wheelchair: "This is Jacques." His grey hair is falling over his eyes, and he's shaking when he raises his glass to sip his drink. "His two o'clock," she says. "Then he's cut off until six."

"He's a good guy," she says. "He was always good to me." Talking as if he's not in the room, or else he's dead. She asks how the drive was and offers me a beer. When I say no thanks, she gives me a ginger ale. I sip and try not to spit it out.

"From when I had the flu," she says. "But I think it's still good."

The kitchen is slanted, and I wonder if Jacques's chair will roll forward. I tell her that the roads were icy and I lie about the ginger ale. "It's fine," I say.

/ / /

THE BATHROOM IS wood panel and there's an old-fashioned ringer washing machine between the green tub and matching toilet. On the tank there's a yellow knitted poodle spare-toilet-paper cover that's grey with dust. On the wall, a ceramic cardinal, a blue jay, a crucifix, and two plaques: LOVE IS NEVER HAVING TO SAY YOU'RE SORRY and STAND CLOSER—IT'S SHORTER THAN YOU THINK.

"So, are ya married?" she asks, when I come out. "Do you have kids?"

"No and no," I answer.

"Oh," she says, putting her beer down on the kitchen table. "You didn't meet the right girl or what?"

"Or what," I say.

"Oh," she says.

"Oh," I say back, and then there is silence except for the toilet running. The old man is asleep in his wheelchair. His empty glass is in his hand and his head is hanging forward.

"You look like your father," she says.

"Sorry about that," I answer, and we both laugh.

"He was a looker," she says. And glancing over to make sure the old guy is asleep, whispers, "A real looker."

"So were you," I say.

She looks down at her hands wrapped around the glass. They are cracked and dry. "I've washed a lot of pots in that kitchen over the years," she says. "Did you ever figure out how to sleep at night?"

"Meditation," I say.

"I take pills," she says, sips the last of her Molson. "Go flick the handle, will ya."

I feel her eyes on my back as I walk to the bathroom. I

jiggle the handle on the toilet tank. It sighs, and stops. I hear her twist off the cap of a fresh beer.

"Do you work?" she asks.

"I write children's books. And I draw."

"Like *The Three Little Pigs* and stuff?"

"Something like that," I say. "I just wrote one called *The Magic Box*."

"*The Magic Bus*?" she says, taking a sip of beer.

"*The Magic Box*," I say. "It's a nursery rhyme: *The magic box has sox in it, the magic box can spin. The shiny box has holes for air, cracks where the stars fall in.*"

"That's nice," she says, fills my glass with flat ginger ale. "You get that from your father," she says. "Boy, could that man tell stories."

I put my gym bag on the kitchen table. "Remember this?" I ask, pulling the black lacquered jewellery box out. "You gave it to me the day you practically burned the church down."

She takes another sip of her beer. We sit side by side at the table, the shiny box between us. After a few minutes I tell her that I put my telephone number inside.

At the door, she thanks me for looking her up and asks how the hell such a chatterbox kid ever grew up to be so quiet. She puts a sandwich in my hand, wrapped in wax paper. "It's peanut butter," she says. "Remember?"

The rain hasn't stopped and the windshield is steamed up, but I can see her motioning me to roll down the window. "Thanks for bringing back the box," she says. "You can put my bones in it when I kick the bucket."

Standing in the rain, shivering, she leans in through the rolled-down window. "Nice of you to take the day off," she says. "Toronto to Montreal is a long way." Shivering more intensely, she asks: "Does he still wear that Aqua Velvet crap?"

Who's he? I wonder for half a second. "What do you think?" I answer.

"Thought so," she says, walks back to the leaning-to-one-side house.

/ / /

HER MAKEUP IS heavy, she looks tired. She is worrying lots—not about Bill, about money. Millions and millions, the paper says. "I'm worried about saying the right thing in the right place to the right people," she tells Bill. Her voice is raspy from all the talking. She's more Right than McCain when it comes to making money vote, says the paper. Hillary with bags under her blue eyes, and a few post-menopausal whiskers on her chin, looks at Bill's back as he walks tall and straight in his fine black shoes across the checkerboard floor to the door that leads to the garage and his car with jazz CDs and warm leather seats.

/ / /

THEY ARE PLOWING the parking lot behind Montreal General. There's a small mountain of snow on the Dumpster outside her window. Her skin is yellow and her stomach is swollen.

She's on her side with the beer bottle hidden under the blanket. The doctor says it's cirrhosis of the liver.

When he leaves, she says, "Thanks for sneaking it in." Taking a sip, most of it rolls down her chin.

"The world always seems peaceful after a snowfall," I tell her.

"Now don't go getting all sissy on me," she says.

/ / /

WE MANAGED TWO years of getting to know one another again. She even stayed sober the time she came to visit me in Toronto. The day I picked her up at the Greyhound, I was happy to announce that I had stocked my fridge with Molson.

"I don't drink no more," she said. "My stomach hurts."

/ / /

I PUT THE jewellery box in the snow, reached up to the wooden door with both hands. As I touched the handle, someone leaned across my shoulder and pulled the church door open—it was the grey-coat lady, her face covered with snow and icicles. She patted me on the head and walked past me, down the side aisle. No more pink-lipstick-note fire, the smoke had blended with the incense, the priest had disappeared, and I didn't know where to go. My eyes focused in the dark, and I thought I saw the grey-coat lady kneeling in front of a statue of a woman with a beard and a fiddle. I moved closer.

The statue was of a bearded woman, she was looking up to heaven, the plaque at her sandalled feet read: *Wilgefortis—disencumbered of her Godless husband*. "It's a blessing to be ugly," said the bearded lady, getting up off her knees.

/ / /

DOWN THE STAIRS I slipped and fell, slid through the snow, all the way to the bottom of the hill where I had left her. In the snow was the messy shape of where my mother had fallen, like a snow angel or a ghost. I saw the Côte-des-Neiges bus going in the right direction so I unzipped my coat and shoved the box under my sweater and ran for the bumper. With snow and slush in my face from the tire, I could hardly breathe but hung on to the bumper. There was a bald spot in the road, no snow or ice—I crouched deeper, hung on until Pie-IX station, then I let go. The jewellery box dug into my ribs and the sidewalk burned my face. "Ski-bottine," I told my father when I got home. I learned it from the French kids at school.

"If they taught you to jump off a building would you do that too?" he asked. "And where the hell is your mother?"

/ / /

THE COUPLE SITTING in front of me on the streetcar argue about who's going to win.

He says, "Hillary is in the hands of corporate America."

She says, "Obama is playing the race card."

He says, "Obama is a good guy, just not all that experienced."

She says, "They hate her because she's didn't let Mister Crooked Dick run away with the show."

He says, "The Clintons are has-beens, and Bill lied about Monica."

She says, "That's their business. Besides," she adds, "*He's* not the one running for President."

He says, "Make a bet?"

This is what I like best about the streetcar. The couples talking it out. Reading a book. Sleeping. People-watching out the window. As the streetcar turns into Broadview station, I put the jewellery box under my arm and stand. Grumpy driver brakes hard and I fall against the doors, but hold onto the box. I walk into the subway and down the stairs to the trains. I need to go west to the Yonge line, then south to Union. I need to get on the VIA train to Montreal, it will rock me to sleep. I will wake and sketch for a while, and by the time the train curves into Place Ville Marie, I will be ready. I'll take a taxi to Saint Joseph's Oratory—no Côte-des-Neiges bus for me this time. No bearded lady or snowy mountain. Just the box that feels like three pounds of sand tucked under my arm. She'd get a kick out of that—*Do you think I'm some kind of friggin' football?*

I wait on the westbound platform, the black box digging into my ribs, shimmering and hard, the light of the train staggering down the tunnel.

/ AUTUMNAL /

Now that the leaves have fallen from the tree in front of her house, it's easy for him to see into her bedroom window. She has left the light on. She has cut her hair real short. Short red hair looks brown. She's skinny, looks like a boy, a boy in pink bikini underwear. The rain pounds the garbage can at the side of her house. He has nothing to be ashamed of. Besides, she left the curtain open. She asked for this. The binoculars are cold against his eyes. He focuses toward the light. Can't help himself. He can see the circle—her tiny, pinched, peach-fuzz navel. She got a piercing. Soon she'll want a tattoo.

What are you doing there? A man's voice from behind him? No. It's a futile intervention from inside his head.

He shivers. Summer went fast. Biking through the ravine. Swimming in Rice Lake. Then, in September, him and her, face to face, knee to knee in her father's garden, drinking wine straight from the bottle, passing it back and forth in the dark.

"Auto-man-ill," she said.

"Ah-tum-nal," he said back, putting his shaking hand on her leg.

"Whouseswordslikethatanymore?" she slurred, then giggled.

It wasn't a joke. He had waited a year to show her. He took the poem, folded it in four, put it back in his pocket.

"Feel," she said, taking his hand. Her knee was warm, and undeniably bruised and swollen. "Why would I make something like this up?"

He took another slug of the wine. He felt dizzy. This wasn't the first time she'd told him about her father. He rested his head on her chest, listened to her heart pounding.

Suddenly her father was there. He walked up to them and yanked the bottle from his hand. Mister jock father was wearing boots and hiking shorts.

"You go home, young man," he said.

The father pressed his mountain climber hand into her sunburnt shoulder. "You stay put, missy."

/ / /

IT RAINS HARDER. He can hardly see her through the downpour, but he finds her sitting on the edge of the bed. Her bony back is toward him. The bedspread is old-fashioned—pink with knobby things all over it like cotton candy or roses. His shivering is uncontrollable and he wishes he could keep his hands still. Then, just like she said he would, her father comes through the door, wearing the same stupid shorts, but he doesn't have his shirt on. She looks toward the window, stands close to her father. The father steps back.

Bright lights, car horn, he runs and falls. He drops the binoculars and keeps running until there are no more lights, no more horns or yelling men. He walks and watches his breathing in the cool air, in and out, in and out. *There he is!* Voices from outside his head. He runs again. He runs then walks. He rides the all-night streetcar. Once the rain stops, he gets off at Wolverly, circles back to her house. There is a car on her street. It slows down, someone throws a newspaper at the door. When the paper guy gets far enough away, he sneaks along the side of her house, curves himself into the shadows behind the security light, close to the wall. He knocks over the garbage can, holds his breath. Her bedroom light is still on and the window is open. He waits and listens. At first he can only hear his heart thumping. Finally, her voice: "He wrote some mental poem about us. And I think he put something in the wine and he started to grab me and stuff."

The light goes out. He waits and stares down at his soggy shoes. The eavestrough is overflowing. *Eavestrough, eavesdrop* he rhymes in his head. The stupid father should pull out the dead leaves. He waits in the rain for what seems like a long time. There is nothing to break the steady pound, except her words riding over and under the father's. Her sobbing filters through the screen. "Why would I make something like this up?" she says.

He should leave. Go home. He kicks at the mud. He should stay. He should rest against the brick of her house, listen for something his head can believe. Wait for his heart to stop beating his ribs.

/ TINA /

Everyone knew Bruce was gay. He was the first one waving his arms in the air when Madonna came on the training mix. He was the only instructor, male or female, who lip-synced to Whitney: *I'm every woman, it's all in me.* He was gorgeous and coifed. Every cycling outfit was coordinated, his hair was bleached and streaked. He wore a perpetual tan, maybe even a little make-up that brought out his white teeth and green eyes. And those cycling shorts. Oh my. Oh my. Now *there* was a man who put the span in spandex.

"Take it. Take it. In through the nose, out from your mouth," he'd say. "Take it. Take it. Take the challenge. Up another notch. Take it. Take it. Go for the burn."

So I did. I went for the burn. I never missed a spin class. I went up a notch, and then another. I pushed harder each time. I lost weight and drank protein shakes to replace fat with lean muscle. I took power yoga to keep myself stretched, and Pilates to strengthen my core—I wasn't Wonder Woman but, according to Bruce, I was well on my way.

"Push, Tina," he screamed. "Climb that hill, darlin'," he'd say. "You need to change your relationship to pain. Love it. Squeeze it. Take it. Take it. Push through the burn."

He'd jump off his bicycle to shout orders from the ground, only it was always me he would stand behind. I'd feel his hands on my hips, gently pulling me back. "Arch your back. Use your quads," he'd yell. "Sit back in the saddle, darlin'. Big circles. Round and round. Climb the hill. Take it." Then he whispered in my ear: "Squeeze those gluteus maximus."

One day after class, deep in thought as I wiped the sweat off my bicycle, I felt his hand on my elbow: "Tina . . ." he said, "do you mind staying a minute?" It wasn't really a request, it was a command.

I just about fell over. I felt ashamed, as if I were a child who'd been caught peeing in the public pool. I was positive he'd noticed that I hadn't increased the tension on my cycle for the pretend hill climb. I wondered if he knew that as I peaked on Gatorade and adrenaline, I had been thinking filthy thoughts about him and all the punch he packed into that tight black spandex.

"I've noticed you bouncing around," he said, "side to side, as if you're going to fall off. Get back up here," he said, patting the seat of the training cycle. "Your shoulders must be killing you."

"My shoulders are fine," I said.

But of course he started rubbing them. On one hand, like everyone else, I was positive that Bruce was gay; on the other, I always knew that his hands would find their way to me—I felt, with every cell in my body, his heat and drive. As his strong fingers kneaded my shoulders, my muscles relaxed and I sank into the seat.

He was tall, probably six-five or six-six. He leaned into me. "I'm going for a drink," he said. Care to come?"

I sat up straight, unclipped, dismounted.

"Aren't instructors given some kind of guidelines about mixing with clients?"

"Of course," he said, winking at me. "But we could. Say. Bump into one another at Woody's in twenty minutes or so."

"Woody's?" I asked. "Isn't that a gay bar?"

"Whatever," he said. *Click, click, click* went his cycle shoe clips as he walked across the hardwood floor. "Twenty minutes!" he shouted over his shoulder.

/ / /

"YOU'RE SUPPOSED TO put your real name there," says the overnight receptionist. "The poster's just a hook."

She's referring to the poster above the desk of three young guys—two of them have brown skin and brown eyes, both are pretty; the third guy is blond, a mix of tough and pouty, his shirt undone, his sleeves rolled up. He has gorgeous veins in his muscles and a dimple in his chin. All three guys wear the same nametag: HELLO *my name is Tina.*

"Tina *is* my real name," I say. "I swear." I have been accused of lying a lot lately. "My last name is Galluzzo." I dig around in my purse for my driver's licence. "I'll prove it," I say.

"That's fine, *Tina,*" she says, making no attempt to hide her sarcasm or disbelief. "This is an anonymous service."

I keep digging around in my purse, but there's not much in there except an empty wallet, gum foil, an old tube of mascara.

My licence was suspended in August.

There is snow on the ground.

I'm wearing high heels and a tank top.

I'm checking myself into detox again.

"OHMYGAWD!" BRUCE SHRIEKED, loud enough for people in the street, and at the back of the bar, and down the next friggin' block to hear. I wanted to crawl under my seat. He plopped his bag on top of mine—an exquisite gym bag made of soft green leather. "Is this Miss Tina Turner from my spin class?" he asked. "*Quelle coincidence.*"

Tina Turner was the name he had given me because of my long legs. "So sexy, so long," he said, putting his hand on my thigh one night as he weaved in and out of the cycles, singing off tune, *Big wheel keep on turnin'*...

He was tacky, sleazy, and silly. Still, I rushed to meet him at Woody's—five minutes in the shower, fourteen minutes and fifty seconds for my hair, ten seconds to run the eight blocks down Church Street.

"Darlin', you're smokin'," he said. "This is soooo much better than cycling gear." He was feeling the material of my skirt.

"It really isn't anything exceptional," I said. "Twenty-nine, ninety-five at H&M."

"You showered?" he said.

"Well of course I showered. Didn't you see me at the end of your class?"

"There's nothing wrong with sweat, sweetie."

"If you're in a spin class."

"What would you like?" he asked. I thought about what I would like. I thought about it for a long time and blushed when Bruce pulled his stool closer to mine. My legs were still pink and burning from the class—in his honour, I had taken pain to a new level, climbed the small hill and then the big hill, pumped and pushed for forty-five minutes.

"A double vodka martini," I said.

"Nice," he said. "Very nice."

When the bartender set the martini down, I moved Bruce's gym bag onto the floor. He quickly picked it up and put it back up on the bar.

"Things get stolen in a minute around here." He waved his arm around the bar, which was empty, except for a couple at a window table.

/ / /

IT WAS MY third year at Smart Set Financial—a terrible job that started out good. Nine-to-five quickly became eight-thirty to five-thirty, eight-thirty to five-thirty turned into eight-fifteen to seven. Swampy River, my boss, was killing me. Susan Lakehead is her real name, but I secretly called her Swampy. She drank too much coffee and smoked too many cigarettes. Her breath was horrible and she didn't seem to know that deodorant existed. The worst part was when Swampy River would lean over my shoulder while I was typing. "Hi, Susan," I'd say, looking up at her blurred reflection in my monitor, "Can I help you?" I'd ask. On several occasions, I almost called her Swampy to her face.

Swampy River never answered, but she came back several

times a day to check my work and breathe her cigarette-coffee breath all over the place.

/ / /

GEORGE, MY EX, got hooked on heroin. It was gradual, but steady, and progressively nasty.

"I can stop," he said. "I just like the intensity. It helps with my creativity."

"I can think of healthier ways of being an artist," I whispered in his ear. He was too busy tapping his needle to care about my raised skirt. Too busy to see me put my bra back on and turn on the television.

"You're an uptight, anal bitch!" he shouted as I was getting dressed for work one morning. He was in bed with his head under the pillow. The issue was money, again.

"I think you should leave," I said.

He was gone by the time Swampy River leaned over my shoulder after her first coffee of the day. He called from the subway to ask for money.

"I don't think so," I whispered. I got up and closed my office door.

He called back: "Take the day off, babe." A last ditch effort to get me to bring him money.

Then, when he realized I wasn't giving in: "You have an addictive personality too," he said. "How many spin classes do you do a day?"

"A couple a week. That's a perfectly healthy way of de-stressing when you work. You get it, George. I work. I'm no addict, nor will I ever be. I come from a normal family."

The last comment was an unfair dig. George's mother died of cirrhosis of the liver; his father had jumped in front of the southbound Spadina train during rush hour and spends most of his day in bed or his wheelchair.

"I'm sorry," I said.

/ / /

I CALLED SWAMPY River from detox. We agreed to meet at a Second Cup on the Danforth at seven a.m. "Hope that's not too early," Swampy River said. I could practically smell her coffee-cigarette breath through the phone. "I have an eight o'clock downtown."

She was standing there, arms folded, when I walked in. "On the patio?" she asked, not waiting for my answer. Four feet ahead of me, she was heading for the nearest ashtray. "Let's not get heavy," she said. "When are you coming back to work?"

I had no intention of getting heavy, or of answering her question. I didn't even know why I showed up. I hadn't slept for two and a half days, and Downtown Detox wouldn't let me use the shower.

"Okay," she said. "So you work too hard. People do that, you know." She sat up straight, took a long drag off her cigarette. "I don't want to know what you've been up to. I don't care. You look like shit."

She actually looked kind of soft for once. Her grey hair was curled and brushed. She wore a little blush, and the grey jacket with the pink-flower blouse beneath made her look almost feminine.

"Don't worry, Swa . . . Susan," I said. "I won't get heavy."

"That would be impossible," she said, placing the ashtray on the ground, then lifting her briefcase from her lap to the glass table. As she handed me a long white envelope with the corporate logo in the corner, she added, "You can't weigh more than fifty pounds soaking wet."

"I've been sick," I said. "Some kind of parasite from Mexico."

"Okay, Tina," said Swampy, reverting back to her tough boss-lady voice. "You deserved a holiday. I don't care if you went to Mexico. I don't care if you went to Timbuktu for chrissake, I'm just glad that you're back."

I began shaking. I couldn't stop. Her breath was disgusting. She blew cigarette smoke in my face when she talked. I owed her nothing, but I couldn't keep my hands still, or my feet. "I'll be in Monday," I lied.

"Should I open this now?" I asked, looking down at the envelope.

"You've earned it," she said. "Corporate told me I was rewarding you for bad behaviour. But screw them, Tina, you've earned it. Consider it a bonus for going beyond the call of duty," she said, popping a mint in her mouth.

By nine, I had walked across the Bloor viaduct to the Yonge Street Money Mart.

By nine-thirty, I was in a cab on my way to Dundas and Sherbourne.

By ten, I was counting off twenties into Wolf's grimy hand.

By eleven, the thousand dollars were gone.

/ / /

"YOU'VE NEVER MISSED a single Tuesday or Thursday night," Bruce said.

We had left Woody's and were at my place, sitting on the edge of the bed. The gorgeous leather bag was between us. I knew that he wasn't boyfriend material, but I couldn't help myself. I was tired of being alone. It seemed like months since a guy had even looked at me. *I'm forty, not four hundred!* I wanted to scream. It had been two years since George, and Bruce seemed like a step forward. Not my best step, I can see now, but a step nonetheless. Besides, a live-in trainer, I figured, who all the women think is gay, could be good. Plus, someone with legs like his had to be amazing in bed.

"Not a one. Not a single class without my Bella Tina," he said.

"I love it. I love the music. I love not thinking about my job for forty-five minutes."

"Is that all?" he said. His hand on my leg felt cool, my skin was still burning from the class. Then, when I didn't answer, he asked: "So. Are you a party girl tonight?"

"Not really," I answered. "I have work in the morning."

He wasn't listening though. He was digging around in the green bag and took out a bottle of wine. He unscrewed the cap and offered me a sip. "You work too hard," he said. "I can tell by the amount of sweat you leave on the bike."

"Thanks," I said, "but that's spin-class sweat. You'll have to check out my chair at the office if you're monitoring work sweat." I was feeling the vodka, but took a swig of the wine anyhow.

"I'd be happy to do that, darlin'," he said, pulling out a Madonna CD, a glass pipe, and a pimple-sized knot of foil.

"Is that hash?" I asked, genuinely surprised that a fitness nut like Bruce smoked up.

"Nope."

Then, I could see that it wasn't hash, the colour and texture were all wrong—at least from what I could remember from my high school graduation party.

"Holy crap," I said. "That's cocaine."

"Nope," he said. "Better." He reached for his lighter. "This stuff has you written all over it. Crystal Meth," he said. "Lovingly referred to as Tina."

Tina. Go figure. Who thinks up the names for street drugs anyways? He pulled me closer, his fingers digging deep into my ribs as he wrapped his rock-hard leg around mine. He heated up the glass at the base of the tiny pipe. A small swirl of smoke began to form.

"Like this," he said inhaling. He turned to face me, exhaling, and added: "You're one sexy, hot babe."

There was a time when I would have agreed with him. As

redheads go, I was kind of *hot*. I was fit and my skin had a nice pink glow.

"Is this stuff really called Tina?" I asked, feeling a little dizzy from the booze.

"Yep," Bruce said, holding his breath as he passed the pipe.

All night: swirl, spin, and burn; Madonna full blast on the stereo; Bruce's lip-sync vibration deep inside my mouth.

/ / /

I DIDN'T REMEMBER falling asleep, but I remembered the sex— I was still wired and wanted more. And more. And more. Sometime in the night I drank the glass of water on my bedside table, and at some point Bruce left. It was probably him who opened the window—a breeze pushing the bedroom curtain across my face is what woke me. And the birds. I heard a blue jay and a cardinal—it was all very Alice in Wonderland.

I wished he were with me—pumped and insatiable. The gym bag was on the floor next to my bra. I called his cell, but he didn't answer. He must be at his morning class, I guessed. I debated whether to call Swampy River with an excuse—a migraine, perhaps the changing barometric pressure.

Meth, I found out, made everything sexy. I was strong and confident. No shyness or insecurities about my body. No borders or restrictions. I could see how someone could get addicted. But not me. I made a promise to myself, never to smoke it again. I'd made my point—I wasn't *uptight* or *anal*. I could go to the edge and come back again without getting hooked.

I had a shower. I brushed my teeth and put on my white blouse and black skirt. I thought about Bruce's body, inch-by-inch of him, all over me. I changed my mind and took off the blouse and skirt, put on a pair of jeans and a tank top, reached into the green bag and took out the glass pipe and the small ball of foil. One little puff for the road, I figured. No harm in that. Another for the streetcar ride downtown. No harm in that either. A third for good luck.

"Hi, Bruce," I said, when I finally reached him on his cell. "You left your gym bag at my place."

"It's yours now, darlin," he said. "Go for it."

So I did. I climbed the hill, shot for the peak. When I thought I'd maxed out, I took the challenge up a notch, and then another. *Take it. Take it. Go for the burn.* Bruce's lip-sync voice deep inside—my head spinning, his fine leather bag in my lap.

/ THREE TRIGGERS /

unger. Lack of sleep. Too much coffee. This is how it happens. I'm awake most of the night and around five I say to my tossing-and-turning self, *Claire, screw this.* I make a big pot of coffee and begin obsessing over my nine o'clock presentation and which of my two black skirts to wear—the conservative forty-three-year-old, just-below-the-knee; or, flip those numbers around, the short, sexy, six-inches-above-the-knee, thirty-four—until I notice the clock on the stove says it's 9:15. I straighten my wig and put on lipstick. I rush out without breakfast and, cursing the inventor of high heels, run back for my laptop, then back out again, and just make the streetcar, collapsing with a sigh next to an over-the-top-with-perfume woman in a pink coat. Okay, I lied, there are four triggers. Perfume finishes me off every time. I don't move and within seconds my head hurts and I feel throbbing against my temples. I'm stuck in the zone of Obsession or Chanel No. 5.

Finally it's my stop and I get off the streetcar. Fog hangs over University Avenue—misty, grey—confusion between hot and cold air, not a good sign. I'm behind a young couple. He has the wildest walk—the momentum all coming from his knees, like a Lipizzaner stallion, high strut and prance. She's a pelvis leader with a green Mohawk, her neck sticking out iguana-like. Hand-in-hand in cowboy boots, they walk down the stairs into the subway. I stay close to the green tiles, flash my transfer at the indifferent attendant, and head for the Designated Waiting Area; although I am neither a senior citizen nor pregnant, I know how bad this can get. The overhead light is painfully bright and the benches are too red. The safety line along the edge of the platform, bevelled for the blind, is bumpy yellow. Can't sit, so I stand. Can't stand, so I sit. Can't breathe. Exhale. Stand up. Sit down. I imagine floating down the cool, dark tunnel, the quiet oblivion. There's an explosion, as if the incoming train has crashed inside my head. *Drama Queen, Ninja of Neurosis, calm down, stand up.* I sit with my head between my legs and too-short-for-a-woman-my-age skirt, hang onto my wig, stare at my size-twelve feet.

"Dude. Something wrong?" says a voice, and I can't answer because my centre of gravity is shifting to my stomach. I can see that Iguana Girl senses this, and like a reverse version of her pelvis-leading self, she steps back with her elbows, followed by her stuttering hips. "She's going to chuck," she says. And I do. All over the bumped-ridge, too-bright-for-the-eyes, heaving-with-yellow platform.

"My job makes me sick," I say, wiping my mouth with the dirty Kleenex that Iguana Girl hands me. "Thanks."

Iguana Girl crouches on the platform and digs around in her backpack.

"What's your name?" Lipizzaner Boy asks. There's kindness in his voice.

"Claire," I say, thinking it's nice that this kid's empathy defies his paint-stained fingers and torn jeans.

"Well, it's not the entire job," I say, my stomach tightening up for round two. "It's the E-Resources stuff."

"What's that?" asks Iguana Girl.

"Human resources without the human. Electronic HR."

"E-Claire," jokes Lipizzaner Boy. "Like the dessert.

"That's kind of funny," I say, looking up at Lipizzaner Boy. "Éclair," I add, when I catch my breath.

"Dry heaves are the worst," says Iguana Girl.

"I think she's gonna pass out," says Lipizzaner Boy. "Get her purse."

/ / /

NO BARBIE OR pink frills for me as a kid. In high school, all the other girls would be in the washroom putting on makeup. Not me. Smoking was my thing. That and drawing with numbers. My portraits were like Picassos done in numbers. Sideways eights for eyes. An angular seven for a nose, hooked and falling sixes for hair.

"You're a genius, Claire," my grade nine social studies teacher said when I handed in my assignment all done in threes—the desk legs, the eraser, the digital clock numbers: three thirty-three; the broom in the corner a totem of head-to-toe threes; the wastepaper basket was a teenage pregnancy three. This was enormous praise from a teacher who, a week earlier, had insisted that my parents deal with my attention deficit disorder, only she called it ADD.

I'd sit lotus style in the middle of the football field and smoke. Sometimes I'd feed my sandwich to the gulls or read *The Tao of Physics* back to front and front to back. But mostly, I was glad that I could see far in every direction. It was like being in the wilderness. I loved the field and the fact that I was alone. I zoned out, stayed until my teacher would march across the field, waving a detention slip in the air.

/ / /

"YOU'RE SICKLY LOOKING," my mother would say. "Try a little mascara to bring out those pale eyes."

"My eyes are not *pale*. People don't have *pale* eyes," I'd say.

/ / /

SEVEN IN THE morning. Tuesday. Not too many people. It's a good time of day—the streets look dirty, but in a nice, gritty way. Time for a cigarette. I have a slight Demerol hangover, but the office will be quiet and I'll be able to focus on the presentation that's been pushed back to Friday.

There's a skinhead on Queen with a Doberman. The dog's ribs are visible and it hangs its head as it's yanked down the sidewalk by a black leather leash attached to a studded collar. The ribs are sad and the collar looks heavy, but it's the nose ring, a brassy hoop the size of a loonie, that stops me—that, and a stud pierced into the bottom of its pinned-up ear. That's when I notice Lipizzaner Boy and Iguana Girl working fast with markers on the Britney Spears billboard fastened to the brick wall at Duncan Street. They are wearing cowboy hats and bandanas; Britney is getting devil's horns and big teeth.

"Hey, what are you doing?" I ask, whispering as if I were plotting a murder.

"Éclair," says Lipizzaner Boy, drawing a black moustache across Britney's upper lip. "Did you get your purse?"

By the time I made it into the office, my purse had been dropped off.

"Yes." I said. "I thought you guys had . . ."

"Stolen it?"

Chaos Cowboys came into existence after ticket sales at the Exhibition went through the roof after an *S* was added in front of the *EX* on the posters on all of the Queen streetcars. After that, advertisers realized that an extra letter strategically placed on an otherwise uninteresting word, or an outrageous statement written across Brad Pitt's sexy chest can give a product that extra zip. Lipizzaner Boy and Iguana Girl were baited and busted one night, now they get cash under the table to bring extra attention to street advertising.

"You should come," said Iguana Girl. "See her?" she said nodding at a bus shelter poster of Nicole Kidman advertising Chanel No. 5.

"Hmmm . . . I could do a lot with that number," I said.

"That's the spirit, Éclair," said Lipizzaner Boy. "Meet us here at midnight."

"You're like Virginia Woolf. Only straighter," says Iguana Girl.

I didn't ask about *straighter*.

"YOU WANT TO go where?" my mother asked at my high school graduation.

"The Jack Kerouac School of Disembodied Poets."

"And since when are you a poet?" she said. "A disembodied poet at that."

"They teach painting too," I answered, knowing I didn't stand a chance.

"Paint by numbers?" she said sarcastically.

I started to cry. My normal response to my mother was to stomp away, give her the cold shoulder. But I stood there sobbing. Then I sat on the kitchen floor next to the dog's bowl, and she sat too.

"Listen, sweetheart," she said, stroking my hair that was falling out by the handful. "Your father thinks that telling you everything you want to hear is going to make things all right. I couldn't disagree more. You need a decent education. A good job."

I didn't say a word. I focused on the squares within circles, circles within squares—the floor covered in ugly linoleum.

"Let's face it, Claire," she said, "You're mixed up, obsessed with numbers—there isn't a big market of guys looking for those qualities.

After high school, I enrolled at the Institute of Computer Technology and pulled off *A*s. I took a watercolour course at Royal College and attempted *real* landscapes. The brown trees melting into the blue river made me sad. My red poppy next to a grey rock made me ill. I couldn't concentrate, couldn't keep my mind in the room. Then I met Christopher Ragland, got stoned, and lost my virginity. Not awful, I thought, looking over his heavy body—wide shoulders and a big, woman's butt—not great, but not bad either, an eight. The wedding was nice and the honeymoon acceptable. I buckled down with consulting jobs and built a reputation as a no-nonsense change management expert.

When Christopher left I was lonely for a long time, but hiding in the grey of my brain was hope—tangled up in criticism and rules, but in there, peeking out, a solid nine.

/ / /

"YOU'VE BECOME BITTER," my mother says over the telephone. "You're rigid and angry, practically a shut-in."

"I'm not a shut-in, Mother," I answer. "And who uses words like 'shut-in' anymore?"

"You have no friends," she adds. "You walk hunched over, and your hair is practically all gone now."

"Enough ridicule for eight-thirty in the morning, Mother," I say, fixing my wig in the steamy bathroom mirror. "I'm going to miss the streetcar."

"You're a businesswoman, for crying out loud, why don't you just buy a car?"

"To use your language mother, I'm *saving for a rainy day*."

"There won't be any rainy day if you catch one of those

chicken or pig flus," she says. "That streetcar is nothing but a Petri dish on wheels."

///

I SUPPOSE I should have thanked her for keeping me on the phone. I should be grateful that the College streetcar broke down. If I hadn't been waiting forever, I probably wouldn't have noticed the Salvation Army poster in the shelter. It depicts a sad child sitting on her mother's lap. Sewage pipes run overhead. The room is sparse, like a jail cell. There is a hotplate and one small window, a clock on a table next to the mom, and under the table a pot with chipped plates stacked inside. The chair they sit on has four vertical and one horizontal rung, it casts a shadow like bars. The pattern of fives is repeated everywhere—four lines with a cross on the sink, four lines with a cross all over the wall. Four lines of the sewage drain in the floor, the fifth line is a crayon dropped there by the child. *Poverty Shouldn't Be a Life Sentence*, the caption reads.

Enough, I think, crushing my cigarette butt with my heel. Enough.

///

MY TASK IS to promote electronic human resources software to the downtown hospitals. I am supposed to tell the CEOs that there will be no negative impact, convince them to get out of the red. I could use a surgery metaphor, perhaps a scalpel as a pointing device—*Imagine your deficit like a big, ugly cancer. Initially there will be discomfort, but then you'll go on, be healthier for having endured the cut. You'll have the staffing solutions you need at half the cost. You'll save by linking together—there's strength in numbers!*

I set up my laptop. I straighten out a few of the crooked chairs, put a bottle of Evian in front of each agenda—one two three four five six seven eight, I play Sesame Street boardroom in my head. *Breathe. Stand tall. Look them in the* eye. I smile as the CEOs enter the room and sit, side by side. They return my fake smile with their own. Except Anne Bartlett. As usual, she ignores me. Head down, she clicks away at her BlackBerry.

I stand between the wall screen and my laptop.

"This mouse is out of control," I say, looking around. "It's part rat."

A few of them laugh while I scold my electronic mouse, give it a pretend pat on its smooth grey underbelly.

"This rat stinks," I say. "This job stinks." I can hardly speak, the adrenaline's flowing fast. I grip the scalpel pointer. "I've been working on this project for three years, and that's three too many. You don't care about people," I say. I throw the mouse down on the table, watch it bounce to the floor like a grenade. "You don't care about anything except your six-digit salaries."

I inhale deeply and feel my body lengthen. Tall as can be, I walk out of the room, past the filing cabinets like a gathering of cubed-off eights, down the hallway, and into my office. I take Einstein's picture off my desk, put it in my purse. I roll my chair over to the computer and start typing. *Seven six five four . . . In three seconds I'm out of here for good!*

I pick up my purse and dig around for Lipizzaner Boy's number. "Hey, Dude," I say, not completely convinced that I can pull off street language, but you have to start somewhere. "You know the bus shelter in front of Citytv, the one with Nicole holding the giant bottle of No. 5?"

"Éclair?" he says.

"Yes." I say, "I'll meet you there at midnight."

I drop my keys at reception. I press the button for the elevator, but take the stairs. No hurry. I'll get there. *There's wilderness out there* pops into my head like a herd of elevens. I walk onto Richmond, kick off my shoes—two big feet, ten little toes. I look down the row of trees in planters, the gorgeous line of nines in boxes up and down the street.

/ THE SINGING DRIVER /

Paul Campbell sits at the boardroom table of Buchanan and Taylor spinning numbers in his head. He remembers taking the old combination lock out of his gym bag at San Francisco airport. He was sure that he'd placed it in the grey bin, slid it through the X-ray at security. He remembers the feel of cool metal, the rough, etched-in dashes under his fingertips before he put the lock back in his gym bag. When he returned home, he checked all of the logical places. He checked the bedroom where he had packed, on Betty's side of the bed. In the kitchen he went through the junk drawer, removing her copy of *The Colossus*. He laid it back inside and gently closed the drawer once he'd finished his search. And then he gave up, walked down to the hardware store, and bought the new lock that just won't open.

/ / /

HE STUDIES THE piece of paper with the combination—44-6-51—cracks a joke about dexterity in one's early fifties as Rita, his assistant, sits down beside him.

"You can't be?" she says, lining up her sharp pencils alongside her notepad on the mahogany table.

"I sure am," he answers, sticking his chest out.

Paul is proud to still have a full head of wavy brown hair, proud to be fit and, for the most part, have his wits about him. He doesn't even need to wear glasses for today's audit meeting.

"Well, this isn't working at all," he says.

"Let me," says Rita. "I'm brilliant with numbers."

On her first attempt, the lock springs open. She raises her hand to Paul, who misses the cue and high-fives the empty air.

"How in God's name did you do that?" He reaches across the table, grabbing the lock from Rita. "I've been fiddling with this thing for fifteen minutes."

"Oh, I don't know," she answers. "You have to take your time."

Forty-four. He turns the dial. Six. Fifty-one. And when that doesn't work, he slams the lock on the mahogany table. "Shit-pissfuck!" he says.

"Wasn't your wife a minister?" asks Rita.

"Yes, she was," he answers, wondering why she needs to bring Betty into the conversation. Betty's the one who sat with him every night at seven and prayed to the memory of their son Tommy, who died at twenty-two of AIDS. Betty's the one who fought breast cancer. She's the one who picked out a matching shirt and tie for him to wear at their daughter Kate's wedding when she finally married a decent guy at thirty. It's her voice that he still hears in the morning when he rushes off the streetcar without looking: "Paul Murdy Campbell. Will you please be careful." *Klang. Klang. Klang. Klang.*

"It's a stupid system where people step into the traffic like that," he'd said. "Someone is going to get killed some day."

WHEN THE TTC had their campaign for new blue streetcars, Betty sent an email to www.streetcar.ca. *They have to be red*, she wrote. *It's a tradition, the colour of passion, a symbol of solidarity for the working poor. And reduce the fares—$2.75 is a meal for some people.* Betty was the one who started the annual September sit-in, Fare Fair for Fair Fares, at Queen's Park.

/ / /

"GIVE ME THAT," says Paul. "Forty-four, six, fifty-one." Once again, the lock doesn't open.

"Sir," says Rita, who has been watching over his shoulder, "the combination is forty-four, six, fifty-*seven*."

"It is not," he says. "It's forty-four, six, fifty-one." Then, looking at the stack of eight-by-eleven financial statements piled in front of him, he adds, "There's nothing wrong with my sight. That can't be a seven."

/ / /

SIX YEARS COULDN'T possibly have passed already. They bought organic. They rode their bicycles to their respective jobs, unless it rained too hard or the snow was too deep. Betty to St. George the Martyr. Him to Buchanan and Taylor. On extreme days they snuggled close to one another on the

Dundas streetcar. She had long hair that curled over her shoulders and freckles on her nose and chest. Betty was short and walked leaning slightly to one side. She loved music and was curiously slow about everything. She loved chatting with the streetcar drivers, especially the one she called the Singing Driver.

"Okay, folks," he said, smiling as Betty dropped her token into the collection box. "Squeeze your way back," he trilled.

"He's flirting with you," Paul said.

"He's just being friendly," she said back.

They did yoga every Saturday afternoon on the Danforth. Betty was the flexible one, but he gave it a good shot. After, they'd get a beet juice from the Carrot Common and go for a walk through Withrow Park. They jogged together every other morning from 5:45 to 6:30. They didn't drink. Neither smoked. But sex. Thank God and the angels for sex. They sure made up for all that day-to-day being good under the covers. At least that's how he saw it.

"On a scale of one to ten, ten being perfect, how would you rate your husband's performance in the bedroom?" the therapist asked.

"Seven," she'd said.

Just like that, he'd been reduced to a seven.

"A seven's good, Paul," she said, reaching for his hand.

A sex therapist. It was her idea. As far as he was concerned she was a ten. And he was a ten too. Well, at least, an eight-and-a-half.

"Don't leave," he'd said.

SOME MORNINGS HE would find her sleeping with her head on the kitchen table. "You're using your hair as a pillow again," he'd say, kissing the back of her head, which smelled of chamomile. She would stretch her arms straight in the air and stand. She'd kiss his cheek and move slowly toward the garden. One morning there was a baby raccoon in a box on the floor next to her chair—it had fallen from a tree. Another morning there was a cardinal with a broken wing that she had been feeding with an eyedropper. Then there was that cat. The stinky feral that sprayed the entire house and put fleas in the sofa. He nervously coaxed it out the back door with a chicken leg.

Paul teased that she was the patron saint of the poor and abandoned. Some mornings she wasn't there, nor was she in the garden. Some mornings she was curled up next to the toilet, a bottle of Gravol in her hand, vomit crusted in her hair.

"I'm cutting it off," she said as she steadied herself on the edge of the toilet to stand up. "That's it," she said. "Not another word, Paul Murdy Campbell, about how short hair is 'manly.' "

/ / /

HE HOLDS THE paper at arm's length. 44-6-51. He is certain. Then again, maybe? Maybe that number one has a line across its top. A seven? He'll try. He'll humour his young colleague. 44-

6-57. The lock pops open. Rita stands and claps.

"The auditors will be here any minute," he says.

/ / /

'BETTY WASN'T INTERESTED in a fake breast, or a bra lined with a gel insert. She didn't need to be "sexy" or symmetrical. She had always felt somewhat off balance—this new scar above her top rib didn't bother her in the least.

/ / /

THE NIGHT HE met her on Philosopher's Walk, she was sitting on a bench close to the Bloor Street exit, reading Sylvia Plath.

"Looks interesting," he'd said, a smirk on his young face.

She didn't get up to leave. She froze, her eyes focused on the first line of "Moonrise." Betty-Ann Tucker knew better than to talk to a stranger in the park.

Then he went away. But each night for the duration of her M.Div. at St. Mike's, she sat on the same bench reading poetry, and each night he returned.

"Why Plath?" he asked on the fourth visit.

"She's a wonderful poet," is all she said.

"Toby's on Bloor has great Apple Brown Betty," he suggested.

HOT APPLE BETTY was the name he gave her after their first sleep-over. The part she hated most was the way he got out of bed right after they'd made love. "Must be ready for tomorrow," he'd shouted from the shower. She stayed under the covers swirling her fingers in circles through the milky pool he'd left on her belly.

"Slow down," Betty had asked him on their honeymoon. "We have our whole lives together."

When the kids have grown? When Tommy gets better? When Kate leaves home? When the mortgage is paid off? The timing had never seemed right to leave Paul. Then Betty felt the bump in her breast. At first it was soft, like a lump of por-ridge. *Just my imagination*, she thought, *a little fatty tissue?* Then, it was hard, an annoying pebble she couldn't ignore.

/ / /

"HALF-BAKED BETTY," PAUL had teased her as she lifted her face from the toilet bowl.

"That's not funny," she said, wiping her mouth. She knew that he didn't find it funny either—thirty-one years together and she'd never seen him cry until that moment. He sat be-side her on the floor and wept.

"Not you too," he said. "You can beat this."

AFTER FOUR MONTHS of chemotherapy, Betty had a visitation from the Virgin—not so big with Anglicans, but Betty felt an affinity with the One in Blue just the same. There was no spectacular, over-the-top vision, the way it's depicted in movies, but there was a bright light, and a distinct woman's voice. Mary had consoled her when she was heartbroken over Tommy. Mary had given her permission to cut her hair: *Just walk into the kitchen and get the scissors.* Mary sat with her until the sun rose. She coached her to not drag out the suffering: *It's time,* Mary said.

BETTY LOVED THE streetcars. They reminded her of San Francisco, where she was from. She particularly liked the Singing Driver. When people were slow to move on, he'd say, "Make way. Somebody has a job to get to. Someone else has worked all night." And when it was time to get off: "Caution to the cars," he'd sing as he opened the doors.

EVERYTHING WAS A task to Paul—each event, something to get through. No pleasure. No play. He was always on his way to being someplace else. Paul couldn't be without her for a minute. If the subway was stalled or she stayed after service with a parishioner, he would be pacing the floor when she got home. "Where were you!" he'd yell. He acted angry, but he looked like a frightened child. And his routines. His need to do the same thing week after week, but never anything without her. And the fights they had over that stupid combination lock—he could never remember to bring it with him. She cherished those nights he went to the gym. But no sooner would she sit down with a glass of wine and a book, and the phone would ring. "I've forgotten my lock," he'd say. "Would you mind bringing it over?"

/ / /

HIS FAVOURITE DRIVER was the Detail Driver. "A minute ahead of schedule," he'd say as they pulled up to a transfer point. "Remove your backpacks as you get on and off the streetcar," he'd preach to students. "And take care of your grandmothers in the heat." The Detail Driver would lecture his passengers on the precise nature of heatstroke. Cause and effect. What to do if it happened to you. "Northbound trains on this side of the street. Southbound on the west, same as the traffic on Yonge." And, a few blocks later, like clockwork: "Bay street number six bus, south to the ferry docks."

/ / /

"THIS IS THE transfer I was given," Paul had explained when they got on at Bay after their trip back from Mount Sinai.

"It's expired," said the Detail Driver.

"Well, I'm not paying again. This is what I was given."

"I am sorry, sir, you need to pay, or to get off this streetcar," he said, opening the doors. "I'm not going anywhere until you leave and you've already put me forty-five seconds behind for the Bathurst connection."

"Just give him two seventy-five," Betty said.

When they sat down, Paul told her he respected the Detail Driver, even if he had to pay twice. "He has rules to follow. He's just doing his job."

She rested her head on his shoulder. Betty just wanted to sleep.

/ / /

"MAMMOGRAMS, BIOPSIES, ULTRASOUNDS, metastasized," Paul blurted out to Rita. "She said we'd live to be a hundred. Her meals were always half cooked. I called her Half-Baked Betty once."

/ / /

BETTY SITS AT the kitchen table reading Sylvia. She isn't afraid of death; it's the dying that's killing her. She laughs out loud, puts her hand to her mouth and cries. She's already had twice as many years as Tommy, and Kate has a naturally buoyant spirit, she'll be fine. But Paul?

When they met, he was a virgin. Rough. Awkward. Insecure. An average guy with aspirations of greatness. She never fooled around, but she thought about it. She fantasized about being with someone considerate and slow. She once dreamt about Ted Hughes. He, according to her friends, was the bastard who killed Sylvia. He was the reason for the gas and the stove. In Betty's dream though, he was sexy and thoughtful. He entered her slowly as he kissed her neck. He held her breasts and circled her nipples with his warm fingertips. He held her, stayed with her after they'd made love.

She woke to Paul shaking her. "You're having a dream," he said.

/ / /

"DEAR MARY," SHE said to her chamomile tea. "Dear Mary," she said to *The Colossus* sitting next to the steaming cup. "Dear Mary," she said to the yellow kitchen wall with the rising sun casting shadows against it.

/ / /

THEY COULDN'T FIND a seat on the streetcar, even though it was the Singing Driver, who is brilliant at getting people to move back: "Okay folks, squeeze your way to the back. Someone is going to school. Someone else may have worked all night. Thanks for your cooperation, folks, it's raining outside." The passengers listened to him. They laughed at his comments: "If you're touching the rear window, you've gone far enough." It was raining hard and it was cold—everyone wanted to be inside, but no one was moving. "Make way. Somebody has a job to get to. Someone else has worked all night. Make way," he said, and they gladly obeyed.

Betty was determined. The stop before their regular stop, she plowed her way toward the exit. "For the love of Pete," he mumbled, trying to catch up to her, squeezing past the students blocking the aisle with their backpacks. The doors opened, and Betty welcomed the rain-soaked air. Paul sensed the urgency in her.

"Betty!" he yelled. "Stop!"

But he was too late. *Klang. Klang. Klang.*

The Singing Driver closed the doors the instant she was hit. Her raincoat was red and she was wearing her mother's pearls. Betty never dressed up for her job—she was conscious that she worked with people who couldn't afford nice things. But those were pearls on her neck. Her blouse had come undone, the scar across her chest was visible, pink with the rain beating down on it. Her eyes were silver, like the fender of the car with its headlights shining into them.

Paul pounded the door. "That's my wife out there!" he shouted. But the driver announced that no one got off until the police got there. Paul put his face against the rain-steamed window. Blood pooled around Betty's head. Not a single hair; she'd cut it all off. *Why?* She was thrown across the tracks—facing up to the sky, rain beating down on her. He cursed himself. *Why?*

"Okay, folks," the Singing Driver said. "Be calm, the ambulance is on its way."

Cover her! Paul tried to yell through the window, but only the intention of the words left his mouth.

/ / /

THROUGH THE BLUR of the headlights and rain, Betty could see Paul on the streetcar, his hands pressed against the glass. She felt peaceful and there was no pain. She couldn't hear him, but she could easily imagine the Singing Driver: *Make way, folks! Somebody has a job to get to. Someone else has worked all night.* And just before she closed her eyes: *If you're touching the rear window, you've gone far enough.*

/ ALPHA VARIETY /

t seemed like the right thing to do on his thirtieth birthday. Fisherman's Wharf. Salty air. Rolling streets. The whole *clang, clang, clang,* Judy Garland on the trolley thing. Anonymity—no chance of bumping into Sean from reception (or anyone else he knew, for that matter). Ryan would get out of the city in December. Away from the Christmas crowds and the cold. He'd answer the question once and for all, get it out of his system, live a normal life. Get a girlfriend. Learn how to play golf better than John Marshall. One night. That's all it would take to prove to himself that given the unbridled opportunity to test it out without fear or inhibition, he would be repulsed by having sex with another man.

He would take the Ecstasy that Speedy, from Road Runner Courier, sold him. Getting a package from A to B in a completely unrealistic time was Speedy's specialty, his adrenalin rush. How he kept up the pace was no secret.

"You?" Speedy asked, wired as usual, pointing his gloved finger at Ryan. "Mister First-One-in-the-Office-in-the-Morning, Last-One-Out-at-Night; Mister Button-Down-Collared-Shirt-from-Harry-Rosen; the Suit that every courier hates, except for the fact we know that when the office is closed he'll still be here and we won't have to make a second trip; Mister Pseudo-Jock-Bible-Thumper-Closet-Case-Who-Lives-On-a-Street-Called-Alphamale is going to San Francisco?"

"Albermale," Ryan answered. "I mean, Albermarle."

"Whatever. Here it is. Enjoy."

Ryan nodded toward reception. "This is confidential," he said, taking the envelope from Speedy with one hand, giving him two twenties with the other. "Besides. It's for someone else."

"Yeah, right," Speedy said sarcastically. "And, like, you're going to San Francisco to study the migration patterns of Canada Geese."

/ / /

RYAN GUZZLED TWO beers; smoked a joint, coughing after each inhalation; opened his contact lens case to get the hidden E, and dropped it with a glass of red wine. He put on a black T-shirt and squeezed into a pair of jeans. At the drugstore he bought some gum and an umbrella. He avoided buying condoms when he noticed the cashier's crucifix necklace and the 3-D Jesus behind her head. And when she said, "Have a good time, hon," he turned red.

At first, the rainbow flags and red ribbons in every other window on Polk Street nauseated him. His feet were wet and he regretted not wearing a jacket. After a few blocks, the air turned warm and salty. He felt easy. Ryan stood back and laughed at his weaving self, splashing through puddles in way-too-tight jeans.

In the bathhouse he felt his way along the dark hallway, through the labyrinth of cubicles, each with a single bed, a locker, and a lamp. After circling for a while, he ended up in a blacked-out room that smelled like cigarettes and sweat. He could not see. Someone in front of him loosened Ryan's belt buckle. A tall guy, behind him, reached under his arms and pulled him close. For a few minutes his shirt was on. Then he was floating. Holding and rocking. Some leather guy's legs in the air. His legs in the air. On his back. On his knees. Ecstasy was just like he'd overheard Speedy describe it to Sean at reception: "You fall in love with every person you meet. You don't think of anything except getting off."

The next morning, he put his dirty jeans and torn shirt in his suitcase. He folded the umbrella, flagged a taxi to the airport. That was that. Out of his system. He was disgusted. He knew he would be. He asked the driver to pull over, and he puked on his dress shoes. On Sunday he'd go to confession. He would ask Karen from finance to a movie. He'd tell John Marshall that he'd been on a tour of West Coast Zen-inspired gardens. Suit and tie—his life would be back in order by Monday at nine. *Promise*, he consoled himself as he watched one plane land and then another—none were taking off.

"Promise," he said to the wind that rattled the floor-to-ceiling windows of the departure lounge as the coming-down-hard rain pulverized the American Airlines jet grounded on the tarmac. His headache worsened. Lightning crossed the horizon. Rolling clouds changed shape—black-green tanks transformed into a herd of grey elephants; a rolling hill unfolded, became an enormous crane, fragments of light striking its silver wings. Ryan leaned his head against the window and sobbed.

RYAN KNOWS THAT if he walks up Albermarle to Broadview, takes the footbridge over the Don Valley Parkway, cuts through Cabbagetown, and walks at a decent pace across Church Street, past the *Volunteers Now!* billboard and giant red ribbon outside the AIDS Committee of Toronto, west on Queen without stopping to pick up a coffee, he'll be opening his first email before John Marshall even sets foot in the lobby of 205 Richmond. Some days when he gets to Broadview, he takes the Carlton streetcar, but today Ryan will walk the forty-five minutes to the office. He needs to push himself harder. Snow is melting, the ice is almost gone; for the middle of March it's downright balmy at eight in the morning. There's even a crocus or two pushing through the thaw. So what if he'd rather walk than drive. So what if some people think he's obsessed with working out, allegedly compensating because he's short and, according to some, gay. No one else in the office can bench press their own weight, do a hundred sit-ups without stopping, climb the twelve flights of stairs to reception without breaking a sweat. No one else earns a not-so-bad six-figure salary at just thirty, and almost landed a promotion that would have paid an over-the-top six-figure salary. Screw them all. He'll have to pick up the pace though, if he's going to shave off the time he lost in the bathroom. No aches. No fever, no night sweats or nausea—it must have been something he ate.

Just after the Alpha Variety on Logan with its white bread,

chocolate bars, and blue-plaster Elvis, he passes the house where John Marshall lives with his twin teenage daughters and cuts up Albermarle toward Broadview. Spinner, the Jack Russell from 44, comes out yipping like he always does. Ryan doesn't have time for pet nonsense and remains focused when the dog's owner rushes up to the gate rattling on about some lavender tulip hybrid that's ready to rise from the dirt any day now. He keeps marching up the street, doesn't look sideways or backward, cuts a path with his bare hands through a snake-infested forest for his exhausted, underachieving troops. He chuckles at his military metaphor. Soldiers. Snakes. How adolescent. Ryan shrugs it off. His stomach tightens, his legs weaken. He rushes across the street, hops on the Carlton car. He needs to get to a washroom fast.

/ / /

HE WAS A shoo-in for the promotion. No one else had brought more money into the agency. No one else was there for the long haul like him. Ryan was young, and he had a vision for the agency. He simply had to show up with a smile and answer a few perfunctory questions about an Operational Officer's role at Media Events, an advertising firm fighting to survive against the slick-minded competition. He was the six p.m., John Marshall was the five-fifteen, but he was no real threat—his limited creativity is inspired by his twin daughters. Twins selling gum. Twins selling shoes. Perfect-teeth twins on a double date with another set of perfect-teeth twins to sell toothpaste. John Marshall's notion that people like the "mirror" that a double represents and that they won't reach for meaning in deeper or more subtle advertising is wrong. Ryan has faith that the new generation is not so easily manipulated. His campaigns focus on human emotions, drawn out by our innate desire for connection. Ryan believes this whole Facebook thing is all about connecting in a way that previous generations haven't. His ads focus on facial expressions—one small tear, like a diamond, on a joyful mother's cheek can sell a million disposable diapers. An approving smile on the creased face of a grandmother can sell a hefty inventory of back-to-school outfits.

On his way home after the interview he stopped at Cyclepath. "It's made for the city," said the salesman. "It's light so you get your speed and it's easy to carry, but you don't have to worry about skinny tires getting caught in sewer covers." Almost $1,800. Ryan didn't mind spending money on a good bike; he was sure he'd just landed the job. Besides, it would be good for those days when he didn't want to take the car out of the garage, but didn't feel like walking either. He wasn't convinced though that this "city hybrid" was as spectacular as he was being led to believe, and everyone knows that Toronto is the bicycle-theft capital of the world, so the likelihood of it being stolen within three months was pretty high.

"Quick release tires. Quick release seat." As if on cue, the salesman piped in. "This one's portable. You don't have to leave any of it outside for thieves."

Riding it home, Ryan felt free, as if he were fifteen again.

No job worries, no illness. Bouncing across the streetcar tracks on Broadview, racing along Hampton to Albermarle, he wondered if he could still do the no-hands thing. Of course he could. The hill was steep. He should probably have put his hands back on the handlebars but was pleasantly surprised at his skill level with the new bicycle. He navigated a bump on Grandview with slight pressure from his right knee. As he passed the Alpha Variety, he leaned into the north side of the Logan intersection, raised his arms in the air like Lance Armstrong. *Glory in defeating cancer, shame in contracting HIV*. Out of nowhere, the inner-judgment pierced him like a bullet to the head. The setting sun was excruciatingly bright. The horizon wide and pale, the leafless maples on Logan excessively straight. His feet came out from under his seat and up behind his back, he grappled for the handlebars, his triceps tightened as his legs continued up over his head. A squirrel with patches of fur missing scurried out of the way. Winter salt: except for one small square of black ice, the road was powdered grey. One tilted thought. An instant of self-loathing, and the world in slow motion—salt and gravel in his eyes, stinging his face. First there was a snap, like a bolt of electricity, as he slid under the car, then darkness.

"You're bleeding," said a familiar voice. "Bad."

He tried to get up on one elbow but couldn't. Everything blurred. Ryan found it hard to breathe. It was John Marshall dialling his cellphone with one hand, applying pressure to the bleeding arm with the other.

"No. Blood." Ryan struggled for words. That much he

remembers. He also remembers John Marshall's eyes looking directly into his. The same evasive gold-green eyes that worked with him on the Daffodil and Tulip Spring Garden campaign for six months. Although he had aged a little after separating from his wife last year, for a fifty-something guy, John Marshall, with his spiky brown hair and good teeth, was obnoxiously handsome. "Blood," he had said. Not HIV or AIDS. But John Marshall's eyes had registered the full meaning in that red-alarm word.

"Blood," he whispered back. Savouring the secret, dropping the arm as if it were on fire, John Marshall stepped back. One of the pink-sweater twins kneeled down beside him, covered his legs with a denim jacket. He was warm. Then it was dark.

/ / /

THE NEXT MORNING, cast on his arm, Ryan walked into the office. John Marshall smiled, said the "Big Guy" wanted to see him. "They're making the announcement today," he smirked. He knew that he wouldn't get fired for being gay or HIV positive—not out-and-out fired anyway, but he knew that he wouldn't get the promotion, and he knew that no one would ever admit why. Ryan walked toward the corner office.

Handsome as John Marshall, only an inch or two taller with icy blue eyes, the Big Guy would come out from behind his desk.

"Sit down," he'd say. "Needless to point out your good qualities, Ryan," he'd say. "Why, you put a face to our customer, long before Twitter and Facebook. You've brought tears of joy to our finance department time and time again."

Ryan knew that his days at Media Events were numbered. The Big Guy would fold his arms and look beyond him, out the Bay Street window. Ryan would go from 5' 6" to 3' 6" in two seconds flat. The moment would embody every cliché—there would be a dark cloud and fading light, a turned-over water glass on the messy desk, and a photograph of a decades-younger wife next to a golf-ball penholder.

He'd thank the Big Guy for the opportunity to apply for the job, say that he understood the decision. Ryan would walk out of the office as John Marshall walked in. His green eyes would have a little extra emerald in the sparkle, and there would be something else—when they shook hands, Ryan would feel a wedding band pinch—it would seem John Marshall was back with his wife.

/ / /

ON THE QUEEN streetcar, one twin stands, one twin sits. They both wear low-on-the-hip jeans, both have silver clips in their blonde hair, green eyeliner above their blue eyes, and fake lashes. They smile at Ryan, walk toward the exit: "Say hi to our dad," they say in unison. Both are OCAD students. One of them carries two art folios, the other carries two backpacks. They are connected in the middle by an iPod, one earbud for each. Both girls wear a blue scarf with matching gloves; one of them is wearing a denim jacket with a red ribbon—she looks back over her shoulder at him sitting in the window. She opens her folio and pulls out a piece of paper. She unplugs from the iPod and walks back to Ryan.

"This is for you," she says. "It's called *Albermarle Dude*."

Ryan looks at the drawing. It's him speeding around the corner, in full bicycle gear, almost horizontal with the curb. He is focused and strong. Everything is bursting with energy and life, the trees seem to be moving as well as the cars, the colours are spectacular—green, orange, purple. There are two men in the drawing. Twin Ryans. The one in front is smiling. He's confident, pumped, leaning into the turn. The second Ryan is wearing grey, sad and hunched over.

"You're the guy in front," she says, returns to her sister who is waiting at the exit.

The twins step off the streetcar into the rain. Holding hands, they slide and sway up McCaul toward the college. Ryan feels something like love, or sadness. Everything is slightly off balance, the streetcar shakes and moves forward.

/ TRIPTYCH TWISTER /

Somebody died there. Someone had to have died in that car. There's too much black soot on the windshield, too much metal and glass on the road. There's a skid mark leading up to the turned-over car—looks like the whole thing started from this side of the highway. Before the accident, traffic was moving pretty good. No rain for a change. No workday rush hour. Just a Saturday morning drive to the cottage to celebrate our one-year anniversary. Now we're stopping and Geoffrey leans across me to get a closer look.

"Don't, Geoffrey," I say, when he sits back but leaves his hand on my leg.

"No problem, David," he says, folding his arms, looking away. "But, you're way too uptight for your own good."

"We're stuck in a traffic jam. Somebody's probably been killed. I'm hardly in the mood to fool around."

"Like putting my hand on your leg is fooling around?"

There are three lanes of northbound traffic and three lanes of southbound; the car's in the ditch between. An OPP cop looks through the smashed windshield. We roll forward a few inches. The ambulance is gone and there's no sign of a body. I can't see blood, can't see torn or burnt clothing, but I can see the twisted car in the rearview mirror. I want to stop. I feel sick.

/ / /

AT THE COTTAGE Geoffrey doesn't mind sharing the bathwater

with me. He doesn't mind if I go first while he shaves. He swims naked when we're canoeing. He's the one taking a leak behind a bush when we're on a walk in the park near his place in the city. I call him my hunk-of-nature painter boy.

"Did you see what was dropped on your pillow?" he says into the steamy mirror. I hear a smile in his voice. He seems content for a change. Happy to be out of the traffic.

"I don't want to know what the cat left on my pillow," I say. Gemini is determined to bring her prey into the cottage. She usually leaves a bird or mouse on the sofa or our bed. Most recently, she dropped a small rabbit on the kitchen floor. She's a fluffy tortoiseshell that adores us both. She's gorgeous and seems to know it. *Purrr, purr, look at me*, she seems to be saying, stretched out on her back, offering her soft belly to be stroked. At night she goes from my pillow to his. "You have bunny breath, cat. Get off the bed," Geoffrey says.

I love the way his legs are thick and his enormous calves bulge and knot. I love the arch in his back and the way his runner's ass curves out when he leans closer to the mirror while he's shaving. Taking a deep breath, I slide my head under the warm water. My scalp tingles from the sunburn. Of all the aspects of aging, it has to be going bald that bothers me most. I loved my curls. I loved the way Athena would wrap a ringlet around her middle finger. "You're like one of those Greek gods," she'd said when we first met. Now that it's pretty much gone, I should probably wear a baseball cap or remember to put on sunscreen every once in a while, but

I don't. Instead, I burn and peel and itch.

Geoffrey talks a lot—even when he knows I'm not listening. His voice is muffled. Under the water, I hear *blah blah blah gargle blah blah blah*. When I surface he's moved on to the planned Berlin trip.

"We could go to the Pergamon. There's this show *Babylon and Myth* that looks really great."

"Sounds good, Geoffrey," I say. "Babel on."

"That's kind of ignorant," he says. "What does 'Babel on' mean?"

"Just playing with the word," I say, sliding back under the water.

When I surface he has turned off the water. I don't look at him but I feel the pause, imagine the sneer on his covered-with-shaving-cream face.

"I can't help it," I say. "Sometimes words just shoot out of my mouth."

"But you are interested in the Babylon thing, right? Talking in tongues, hanging gardens, linguistic confusion . . ."

"Of course, sweetheart," I say, as I dry off. "Athena says I'd love it."

"So, if Athena says you'll love it, it's a go?"

"That's not what I mean," I say. I rinse off my body as he taps his razor against the side of the sink. "It is what you meant," says Geoffrey. "And don't you think you could tell her to clean her hairs from the bathroom sink?" He's frowning, dangling the soggy clump of blonde hair that he's pulled from the drain.

"I'll get rid of it," I say. I rip some tissue off the roll, wrap it up, shove the hair into my back pocket.

I don't remember things the way he does. I have a general knowledge of art and history, but unlike him and Athena, I don't remember details. Don't ask me where I was when Kennedy was shot or which one of the Beatles Margaret Trudeau ran off with—or was it one of the Stones? Don't ask me to remember this discussion when we get to Berlin, and how I agreed it was a great idea. Thirty years working in finance and I can hardly remember my pin number. "Your memory is fine, David," he is fond of saying. "Just selective."

"Book the trip, Geoffrey," I say, slipping into my jeans. "Let's not have the ex-wife conversation again."

The bathroom smells like cedar. Being in the tub is my favourite part of staying at the cottage—especially when it's steaming with hot bath and shaving water. The window looks out onto the lake. I put on a T-shirt, bend to put on my socks. My body is pretty solid for fifty-five. I still have abs and my legs are strong from jogging. Geoffrey says, "All the better to squeeze me with." Athena says, "All the better to run away with." Athena, who starves herself for four days, then eats enough for three of us on the fifth. Athena, who perpetually smells like coconut oil because she spends more time on the tanning beds at the gym than working out. Athena, a kind soul, the sincerest person I've ever known.

WE WERE ON our honeymoon, standing in front of Mercury at the Louvre.

"Gorgeous," Athena said.

I had to agree. I wanted to run my hand over the lips, down the smooth chest, and across the bronze ass. I was attracted to the mythology of Mercury and insane about the physical body.

"Gorgeous," I said back.

But that's as far as I would go. I'd never slept with another man, and I would never have crossed that line, never have done anything to hurt Athena. She was beautiful and brilliant.

"Did you know that Athena, the goddess of wisdom, sprung fully formed from her father's head?" I asked.

"Did you know that Mercury is the god of thieves, heralds, and herds?" she asked back.

There was integrity in her voice, confidence and contentment—two qualities I knew little about. She took my hand and squeezed it; the statue between us seemed to lose its glow. I kissed her on the forehead.

"Let's go," I said.

"Let's go," she said back.

Her hand was warm. I could feel her finger bones contract over mine.

IT WAS GEOFFREY'S first trip to the cottage, his first time meeting Athena. She read aloud from Webster's:

Twister: in the United States, a colloquial term for tornado.

Tornado: a localized and violently destructive windstorm.

Twister: describes a roller coaster layout that features many turns.

The Twister Bellapiscis Medus is a triplefin fish.

Twister: a game of physical skill produced by Hasbro.

Athena put the dictionary back on the shelf and placed her seven letters—T-W-I-S-T-E-R—on a triple word score.

"I win," she said matter-of-factly as she bent the Scrabble board in half, funnelled the plastic letters back in the box, and put it back on top of the pile with the other games. She took the Twister game off the shelf, spread the dotted vinyl mat on the carpet, and passed me the board with the red arrow.

"Come on, you guys," she said, slurring her words. "Scrabble's boring."

After three days trapped inside the cottage because of rain, Geoffrey was right in there. No shirt or pants, just his swimsuit. As if by wearing his swimsuit, he could will the sun to come out. No doubts about his physical attraction. Not even a hint of self-consciousness.

At first I held back.

Athena was already on her third glass of red wine. "Spin the dial," she said.

There were some pretty hysterical moments—Geoffrey's

leg over Athena's chest; Athena's leg over my mouth; my arm across Geoffrey's ass; Gemini clawing at the cardboard spinner. We had all kinds of games at the cottage—Scrabble, Mononoply, Yahtzee—why did it have to be Twister? God knows.

"If Geoffrey gets to have his shirt off, then so do I," she said. "You too, darlin'," she said to me, and Geoffrey didn't seem to mind.

He didn't mind when Athena's shorts came off either. He didn't mind when we stopped spinning and the three of us were practically naked, skin sticking to the vinyl. And I'm sure it was him who suggested the bedroom. He said it was all her fault because she's still in love with me. Said he didn't ever want to see her back at *our* cottage.

/ / /

THERE WAS A cellphone on the ground and a purse. A mauve purse with silver glitter. I turned the air conditioner on high, rolled up the window as we inched forward. It was thirty-four degrees, and it wasn't even noon. I saw what could have been the heel of a woman's shoe—a stiletto that looked like a lipstick or a lighter—and a few inches away, the other shoe.

"When was Athena leaving the cottage?" I asked Geoffrey, who hadn't said a word for five minutes.

"I don't know, and I don't care," he said, rubbing his hands together. "Could you *please* turn down the air conditioner?"

IT WAS ATHENA'S fault. She was the one who dragged me to the Queer As Pop art show on Church Street. She was the one who dragged me over to his booth with the enormous paintings.

"This guy's an obsessive painter," she said. "That's why his paintings lack emotion—he won't settle into his art. He's only so-so," she'd said, taking my arm, leading me over to his booth.

"He's doing some things with myth that I think you'd like," she whispered.

All of them were triptychs. "Like Warhol," he said. "Only with one box missing."

They were terrible. Proportions were all wrong. The painting had no focus. No emotion. Flat, urban depictions of Zeus, Aphrodite, and Hermes. But how could I say no to those sexy brown eyes and scruffy young face.

"I'll take this one," I said. "How can I reach you?"

"SURE, BABY," I said, reaching across to turn off the air conditioning. "No problem. It's hard to tell, but does that car looks like Athena's?"

"There's two million cars on this highway, David. Do you really think that particular pile of twisted metal belongs to her? It's not all about Athena, you know."

The guy in front of us slammed on his breaks.

"Fuck," Geoffrey said, wiping coffee off his paint-stained jeans.

/ / /

"HE'S A LITTLE self-centered, and a bit of a sex maniac," I'd told Athena, two weeks before the accident. "But he gets over things quickly and is a pretty decent guy," I'd said.

We were at her place, sipping red wine.

"Except he always forgets my birthday and expects me to fill up the gas tank in his piece-of-junk car."

I dropped the key to the cottage in her hand, told her to leave it under the doormat when she leaves. It's part of the divorce deal—she gets access to the cat and the cottage.

"You're one hot little blonde," I added, touching her hair.

"It's funny," she said, ignoring my flirtation but standing tall, teasing her hair with her fingers. "You used to forget *my* birthday. As for the gas thing, you were always the one who left the tank empty." And covering her eyes to add emphasis to her last comment: "I'm not interested in your goings on in bed, but I can't imagine how a 'sex maniac' could be a problem for you."

"Have another drink why don't you, Athena," I said.

"David, you're getting old," she said. "Fifty may be the new forty, but forty's no walk in the park either. I don't know why I care, but you're pushing that kid away," she added, staggering to her feet.

"He's no kid," I said. "He's in his twenties."

She didn't have to say a word, the raised eyebrow said enough.

Her eyes are amazing—dark brown like Geoffrey's, only deeper, more liquid. She has a tiny little dancer's ass and long, long legs. You can tell that her hair is dyed because of the black roots, but blonde suits her, and so does the big jewellery and lip gloss. We'd first met at a Greek restaurant on the Danforth. She was there with another grad student, a girlfriend. After university, we moved into an apartment on the Danforth, ate souvlaki once a week, fought and fucked and fought—for thirteen years.

"You're still gorgeous," I said.

"You're a pig who has no business flirting with his ex-wife," she said, pointing to the door. "Especially after you've dumped her for a guy."

/ / /

THE TRAFFIC EVENTUALLY freed up. Little by little, cars gained speed. The guy in the SUV in front of us was riding his brakes so I changed lanes. As we came up beside him, I saw that there were actually three of them in the vehicle—a group of tough guys in their early twenties. The two passengers, one in front and one in the back, rolled down their windows. "Hey daddy . . ." the one in the back said, ". . . What's the big hurry, faggot."

"Fuck you, asshole," Geoffrey said while I stared straight ahead.

"Don't," I said. "Don't encourage them."

The SUV cut in front of us, slammed on the breaks again, then sped off.

We'd had these discussions before. Geoffrey said I should come out of the closet, get Athena out of my head. He wanted to hold hands on the street and kiss in restaurants.

"This is cottage country, David," I said. "Rednecks and religion."

"Forget it," he said. "They could have killed us!"

/ / /

GEOFFREY PAINTED THE three of us underwater. He called it *Triptych Twister*. Me in the left panel wearing a suit, tie, and boxer shorts with my penis hanging out—only it looks like a second tie. Athena is in the middle, holding an ornate shield with an image of Medusa in relief. An owl is perched on her shoulder, her breasts are massive and buoyant. He painted his handsome self in the panel to the right of Athena, with his gorgeous ass facing out, wearing nothing but a pair of gold Nikes. He's looking back over his shoulder: suspicious, brush-cut sexy, like a soft-souled skinhead. Athena holds a large silver ball, a giant pearl that she raises to the surface of the green-blue water. There's a door between each frame of the canvas. The gold knob has been removed from Athena's door; it's being crushed by my foot in a black brogue.

"Black shoes and boxer shorts, I look like an uptight business goof," I said.

I'm carrying the briefcase that Athena had bought me, and a school of goldfish swims out of my wide-open mouth. The three of us are posed on a vinyl mat that floats like a giant stingray—there are circles on it, each row a different colour: red, green, yellow, blue. I am holding the spinner—right foot, red circle. There are no flames in the painting, but plenty of steam—the water is swirling, Geoffrey's emotional breakthrough: twisted and hot.

"Why fish from my mouth?" I asked.

He kissed me on the lips. "Fish are less lethal than bullets," he said.

There was strength in that kiss. He tasted like paint—sticky, acrylic.

"Why is my penis tied in a knot?" I asked.

/ / /

ON THE PILLOW, there's a box. A small blue box with a big white bow. Geoffrey comes into the bedroom, looking tanned and wet, water pooling around his feet.

"Open it," he says.

My throat tightens. I don't pick up the box, and I can't believe what's about to leave my mouth: "You have no idea about marriage," I say.

/ / /

IT WAS GEOFFREY'S turn to drive. He was babbling about the

idiots in the SUV, the weather, the accident, and the planned trip to Berlin. Then, out of nowhere: "Will you marry me?" he blurted out. His eyes were focused on the road ahead. The traffic was moving fast.

"You're joking?" I said. "A wedding with family and a priest and the whole bit?"

"I'm serious. I want to share my life with you. I want you to know that I don't give a damn about the difference in our ages."

"I'm not worried about my age," I said, turning to face him.

"We're in this together. I love you, David."

"Blah. Blah. Blah," I said. I could hear myself sounding like a ten-year-old. I heard each *blah* like a thrown dart. I saw his face turn red and felt my body being forced into the back of the seat when he pushed his foot down on the gas pedal, but I didn't stop, I gave him a hundred good reasons why we shouldn't get married.

/ / /

I APOLOGIZED AND told him that I'd think about it, and by the time we got to the cottage, things had settled down. The sun on the waves, the sandy path leading down to the water, even the new shed that we'd built to keep our scuba gear in looked like precious gold.

Geoffrey shouted from inside: "It smells amazing in here."

I joined him in the shed. It did smell like cedar. I took off his shirt and then mine. I took off his belt and undid his zipper. It was the kissing that got me, the kissing after the fight, and the passion and the tongue. That was the beauty of Geoffrey—whatever crap I threw at him he forgot about in ten minutes.

There were no pillows or pillow talk, only knees-burning-on-the-sandy-floor passion. I couldn't stop myself when he asked me to stop. He wanted to talk. He wanted to be serious and romantic. He wanted to go back to the question he'd asked in the car. I put my hand over his mouth. I held him close.

Athena and I bought the cottage together. It was going to make things better, bring romance back to our marriage, get her away from drinking and me away from the job.

"We'd better get cleaned up," Geoffrey said, bending down to pick up his clothes from the floor. "I'll shave while you have a bath."

"Sounds like a plan," I said. "Athena said she'd leave the key under the mat."

/ / /

I'M SURE IT'S a telemarketer. It's seven o'clock. They always call just as you're starting to relax after dinner

"I'm busy right now," I say, hanging up the telephone. "I was a little abrupt, I guess," I say to Geoffrey who's curled up by the fireplace with a book.

"You're always a little abrupt," he says.

"No, I'm not."

"Whatever."

"Is that all you thirty-somethings say? *Whatever*?"

The second time the telephone rings I use exaggerated politeness. "Yes. It is he. How may I help?"

Geoffrey rolls his eyes and looks down at his book.

"You found my number in her book? Yes. I understand. Southbound 404. I'll come right down."

Geoffrey puts down the book, stands beside me.

"It's impossible. It's impossible. Impossible," I say.

/ / /

THREE WEEKS AFTER Athena's funeral. We've gone for a swim and Geoffrey runs ahead of me back to the cottage. He shouts from upstairs.

"Guess what's on your pillow?"

"Not again," I say. "I'm not coming up there until you get rid of that thing."

There's a pause, a short silence before I hear: "That's it," he says, "I wanted this thing to work."

I catch the past tense "wanted," but let it go. I walk into the bedroom and watch him dry himself off as fast as he can, then throw the towel on the floor. He walks over to my side of the bed, takes the ring box off the pillow, pitches it out the window. I look out in time to see Gemini run under the shed. I think I should say something, but I can't. *Cat got your tongue* comes to mind and I smile.

"This is no joke," he says.

"I suppose," I say back, but I don't stop him.

He'd worn a suit and tie to Athena's funeral. He'd sat next to me and took the curses and dirty looks from her family. He'd finished his painting and hung it in the cottage.

He throws a few shirts and jeans into a suitcase. He tosses his paints and brushes into a plastic bag. Downstairs, he takes the triptych off the wall above the fireplace. He's trying to do it all at once—the suitcase, the paints, the brushes, and the painting. It seems strange to be helping him, but stranger to watch him struggle alone—I carry the suitcase across the yard. Together, we place the painting in the backseat of the car. The opportunity to stop him comes and goes. *Dinner's almost ready!* I could shout, but don't. *It's hamburgers!* could buy me some time. *Stop. Don't go*, would be more definitive. Instead, I watch him drive up the dirt road, away from the lake and cottage.

"You'll miss me," I say to the back of the car—words like goldfish flowing from my big mouth.

I put my hand in my back pocket, feel the clump of tissue. I unfold the thin white layers—inside, woven together like a tiny, tight nest, the gold strands of Athena's hair. I sit where I was standing. I stare at the lake, hang onto my feet, rock back and forth, in time with the waves.

/ THE GIRL ON
THE ESCALATOR /

She has her head down, but Christopher can see that her face is beautiful and her hair is black and shiny as ink or oil, and long, hanging down past her waist. He is sure that she's only in her teens. Standing still, yet moving, side-by-side, part way up the escalator, under the Michael Snow life-sized Canada Geese, she looks over at him—her eyes strong, charged. It's his job to notice details. Christopher can usually come up with better descriptors than "beautiful" for a face (even though it is), or "ink or oil" for hair (even though it does shimmer like liquid). Some words just take longer than others.

Actually, it isn't her beauty that first catches his eye, it's her orange sweater, identical to the one he is wearing. Her sweater and her big belly. He is killing time on the escalator because he can't make up his mind about work, and he can't make up his mind about what to buy from the food court. He gets accused of this all the time—of not being able to make a decision, moving too slowly, living in La La Land.

Christopher calls his orange sweater his Happy Guy sweater. He also has a navy sweater that's his Grumpy Guy sweater—he usually wears it when a project nears its deadline and he's behind schedule. And a grey one—most Grey Guy sweater days are rainy and cold in the fall or winter.

The Eaton Centre atrium is bright with October light, that really great light that comes when summer smog begins to disappear and the air begins to smell fresh again—buckets of sunshine shimmer through the skylights, over the wings of the about-to-land Canada Geese. Both of the up escalators are heading toward the second level. *Chicken wrap or souv-laki on a pita?* he thinks.

Ron Ingram taps him on the shoulder. "You're thirty-five, not sixteen," he says. "Are you high?"

"Where did you come from?" Christopher asks.

"You'd better get back to the office. Stephanie's pissed."

"Hey, Ron. Two escalators going up side by side. How weird is that?"

"You have to watch out for this kind of phenomenon," Ron says. "If a butterfly flutters its wings in Oakville, the end re-sult could be a tornado in Austin."

Ron Ingram tells Christopher for the third time in one week about what he calls the Newtonian Effect. "For every action there's a reaction," he says. "It all boils down to physics. Two parallel escalators going up change the scale of things."

So it's no big leap to figure out that something pretty phe-nomenal happens next. The tall blonde woman, with lace-up sandals and the Williams Sonoma shopping bags, falls into the toddler holding the pink-haired doll, whose mother grabs her arm and lets go of the baby carriage for a half second and, in all the confusion and tumbling, crashes into the girl in the orange sweater. And there isn't a sound from anyone until the little boy at the foot of the escalator with his hand on the red Emergency button gets his fingers slapped by his mother.

"I'm heading back to the office," Ron says. "That kid's screaming is going to cause an avalanche."

SHE IS VIBRANT. The orange sweater is raised over her belly, and her face is illuminated by the blood of pushing and the blood of pulsing beneath her tanned skin. There are streams of people and of water, pooling around her feet; men and women and children gather—from where Christopher is kneeling, they are bright as Chinese lanterns, swirls of moving light and colour. The up escalators are blocked off with yellow streamers of Emergency tape. A human partition forms, four or five people deep and growing, around the bottom of the escalator. Clouds rush outside the glass ceiling, and beyond all this chaos are the silent and still stars—it is daylight so Christopher can't see them, but he knows beyond daylight, beyond the moving stairs and ever-shifting Canada Geese, the stars are there, waiting for dark.

The girl on the escalator is on the floor. She lets out a big sigh and holds her belly. "Breathe," people are saying. *Breathe.* Her leg is bleeding, although the cut looks superficial, and in the greater scheme of things happening, a hurt leg is nothing.

"What's your name?" she asks, yanking on his sweater, trying to catch her breath.

"Christopher," he answers. "What's yours?"

"Katie," she says. "Katie Watson."

He is kneeling beside her, holding her hand. How he got there before anyone else, he's not sure—fast is not his forte. He only remembers that with a big heave and a sideways lunge, he vaulted over the escalator's black handrail in time to catch the back of her head before it hit the floor.

"Breathe," he tells her. "Breathe."

"Push," someone shouts from within the crowd. *Push.*

The girl on the floor seems to be doing both in rapid succession. *Pant. Pant. Pant. Scream.* "Can you see her?" she asks.

"Are you sure it's a girl?"

"I'm positive," she says. And with that, the crown of the head and the first curly hairs come through, followed by two little pink ears.

"Dark hair like yours," he says.

"Oh!" she screams and pushes until the tiny wet shoulders emerge and then the entire baby jettisons onto the floor of the Eaton Centre. And after a little while, the placenta arrives, attached by the red and blue umbilical cord, long and twisted like a kite string. One of the paramedics places the placenta on the baby boy and all seems well—ten fingers, ten toes, and a tiny heart that seems to be pounding just fine.

/ / /

ON NAVY SWEATER days, Christopher stays inside with a book, or else he rides the subway. The subway's not a bad place for such days. The trains are interesting and he likes being with the crowds. His favourite cars are the old clunkers with orange vinyl seats, glossy orange doors, taupe walls and floors. He usually doesn't talk to anyone, cherishing the solitude of rattling trains and anonymous people. He likes the smells on the train: someone eating a curried sandwich, someone else drinking coffee, the girl sitting beside him chewing spearmint gum.

/ / /

AT WOMEN'S COLLEGE Hospital, Christopher calls work and asks Ron Ingram to tell Stephanie he isn't coming back to the office.

"But the Jorgenson case is coming up," he says.

Christopher feels that he has no choice, the universe is colluding to get his attention. Like a pinch or a nudge, his endless walking in circles seems to have some kind of relevance.

"Don't torture me with decisions right now, Ron. Tell her I'll get around to Jorgenson soon enough."

/ / /

"YOU COULD CALL him John?" he suggests. "After John Lennon."

"Be careful with the name you give a kid," Katie Watson says. "All names are loaded with the parents' agenda."

"I knew a girl who was born on December twenty-fifth," he says. "I used to call her Christmas Girl."

/ / /

THEY LIVED IN Scarborough. They were fifteen, walking to school.

It always seemed to be raining on the first day back. Christopher said they should smoke a joint, even though he was worried because first class was French.

"I'm pregnant," Noelle said. "And you're too young to be a father."

"I'm too young to die. Your father's going to kill us," he answered, trying not to overreact, trying to be cool.

They walked some more and decided to get stoned anyhow. *One joint isn't going to kill the kid*, he reasoned. And it drizzled and then it rained hard as they walked around the school trying to decide what to do. But they made it on time for French and got sent down to the principal's office for being *Très, très disruptive*.

"Are you two high?" asked the principal, and they both laughed until they cried. Then Christopher walked her home and left her there, at the kitchen table with a coke and a bag of salt 'n' vinegar chips, waiting to tell her father the news when he got home from work.

"What did he say?" Christopher asked when she called later.

"Not much. He just kicked me in the ass and called me stupid," she whispered.

"He kicked you!"

"Not really hard. It was the side of his boot."

"What else."

"Nothing else."

"But you're going to have it, right?"

"Yep."

"Just like that. You're going to be a mother."

"Sort of," she said, and then she cried a little. "I have to go to Wolfville, and give it up."

"Oh," he said.

"Oh," she said back.

/ / /

THEY WALKED TO grade nine holding hands. Noelle looked like a grown woman. She wore nice maternity clothes and a little makeup. He liked the way she smelled, and he kissed her cheek, the way he thought a husband would kiss a wife. Although she was getting bigger, she looked shorter, and her legs wobbled like they were going to give out. The other girls whispered; some even called her slut to her face.

"Big as a bus," said the school guidance counsellor.

"Broken-down bus," Noelle answered, sighing as she eased herself into a chair next to Christopher, who already had his face in his hands, his shoulders moving up and down as he rocked back and forth, refusing to look up.

/ / /

THEY DIDN'T GET stoned, but still listened to Zeppelin. They walked down the stairs into the cool dark of Greenwood station. "Stairway to heaven," she said, walking slowly. They took the westbound train to Broadview and walked over the Bloor Street viaduct.

"Heaven," he said, looking across the Don Valley.

"Heaven," she said, pointing to the expressway. "Look at all those cars, and all those people inside them, probably going somewhere cool like New York or Montreal."

"River to heaven," he said, pointing to the Don.

"Train tracks to heaven," she said, pointing to the tracks as a CN train cut between the river and the highway heading east.

"Let's keep it," she said. "I'll go to Wolfville and pretend I'm going to give it up, but when Grandma Lewis is sleeping, I'll sneak out with the baby to the bus station."

"We could meet in Montreal."

"I'll find a cheap place," she said.

"Do you have a roach clip?" he asked. She dug around in her backpack and came up with a pair of eyebrow tweezers.

"How do you feel?" he asked.

"Tired," she said. "Worried."

Two weeks before the baby was due, she left for Wolfville on the train. Christopher said he didn't think he should skip any more classes, so she went alone.

/ / /

BEFORE THEY LIVED in Scarborough, they lived in Montreal. They lived on Eighteenth and Dorchester. Christopher had a younger sister. Her name was Charlotte, after the spider book. His mother taught kindergarten. They lived in an apartment on St. Cyr Street above the concierge. The two-storey apartment building was next to a mansion, the only one in the east end. The owners didn't like them very much.

"*Bonjour*," he'd say, practising his grade four French.

"*Bonjour*," the rich man said back, but that was it.

Christopher only saw the rich neighbour's wife once. She was walking along Crescent Street with his father, who was wearing his police officer uniform. The wife and his father didn't see him coming along the sidewalk. She was crying. Maybe he'd given her a ticket. Maybe someone had stolen her purse. What did he know?

Then they had to move again.

/ / /

"DAD," HE ASKED, his head still buzzing from listening to "Stairway to Heaven" full blast and from smoking half a joint. "What would you do if Noelle got pregnant?"

His father headed straight for the telephone. "Is Noelle there?" he asked.

"I'd give you the boot," he answered, as he slammed down the receiver.

"Charlotte, go to your room." His mother's mouth came unhinged. "Christopher, what did you go and do?"

Before he could answer, his father was standing with his finger pointing to the door.

"Can I at least pack?" Christopher asked, but his father just pointed, as if he were a traffic control officer, standing red-faced at a busy intersection, a silent whistle blowing in his mouth.

"WHAT DO YOU do for a living, Christopher?" asks Katie Watson.

"I'm a computer forensic guy," he mumbles.

"Sounds fascinating. Do you like it?"

"Somewhat. And what do you do . . . other than make babies?"

"I'm a landscaper."

He wonders why no father was called from the hospital. Why there's no ring on her finger. "Do you have a boyfriend?" he works up the courage to ask.

"Nope." The nurse comes in and takes the baby back to the incubator. "Christopher? You're avoiding my question."

"I like my job so-so," he says.

And that's the way the conversation goes for twenty minutes. Then Christopher says he has to go back to work, but he wanders around the hospital for hours—starting at the top floor and working his way down. He sees people with casts raised in the air and bags with plastic fluid lines dripping into their arms. He sees people vomiting into silver bins and people sleeping peacefully in their rooms. He looks at the babies in the window on the second floor, and then he goes back to the waiting room. A young dad is there, reading *The Cat in the Hat* while his son reads a Spider-Man comic.

He sits for a while, then he goes back to Katie Watson's room where he has to wake her because she is asleep with the baby in her arms.

"Before I go," he says, sounding more like Eeyore than Christopher Robin, "don't you think it's going to be hard doing this all on your own?"

Katie Watson looks at the baby boy with dark skin like hers, and tiny red lips and handsome eyes, wrapped in a blue blanket. She holds him close and kisses his cheek.

"Yes," she says, as the nurse places a glass of water on the plastic tray in front of her. "But he's a Libra. It will all work out."

"What made you think this one was going to be a girl?" he asks.

Katie Watson sits on the edge of the bed, one hand holding the glass of water and the other waving in the air.

"Because I wanted a girl."

"Oh," he says.

"Oh," she says back.

/ / /

HE DIDN'T THINK Noelle would really go to Montreal; besides, he couldn't afford it. But he swears he would have found her once he'd wrapped his brain around the whole thing. Christopher would walk and think about it while he worked as a busboy at Fran's. Then he got fired for being too slow. Then he walked and walked and walked and thought about college. He walked and thought about it some more until he found and lost his first I.T. job, and then the next.

"You like digging around," his boss said, as he handed him

a pink slip. "You're slow, but smart and persistent. Go into forensics or something."

So that's what he does. Christopher walks and thinks and sometimes he rides the subway and thinks about how he is going to tell the I.R.M. boss that, yes, his Vice President of Human Resources spends most of his day on porn sites. Or the Jorgenson Case Management agency—how will he tell them that, yes, their best case manager deleted half the files belonging to the Crystal Meth overdose case?

Sometimes he rides the trains for hours, then he goes back to his job, Christopher Robin, Computer Forensics Expert. His boss, Stephanie, is pretty fair. She just wants the job done on time. She's told him this on several occasions. He always assures her he'll get around to it. Once he came into work and there was a cardboard model of a castle tower on his desk. *To Christopher, from Stephanie.*

"What's this?" he asked.

"It's a round to it," she said.

"A round turret? Why a round turret?"

/ / /

THE HOUSE WAS surrounded by hydrangea bushes and each of the rooms had a vase. Each vase had fresh cut flowers, some of them made her sneeze. Each of the rooms was a box painted mint green, pink, or yellow.

Each street led to the harbour and all of them ended in a pile of rocks. Each rock seemed too big or too small for her to sit on. The harbour emptied twice a day—apparently because of the high tides of the Bay of Fundy. It's the smallest harbour in the world and Noelle didn't have much else to do except sit on a rock and watch it empty and fill and think of her options. Plans A, B, and C. She could finish high school and then go to Acadia. She could finish nothing in Wolfville and take off with her baby to Montreal and meet Christopher. She could wait for the harbour to fill again, but she thought her water just broke and it was a long walk back to Grandma Lewis's.

Each street went up the hill and all the rooms were empty when she got to the house. Each minute was an hour and each contraction was a knife in her back. Then a flood of pain broke her open, and her daughter was sliding into her grandmother's arms.

"Ten fingers. Ten toes. A beating heart. Looks good."

"Where did you come from?" Noelle asked her grandmother, who didn't answer. Each second was an hour and she wanted to sleep.

Then, each minute was a regular minute, and each hour dragged on as she thought things through. Grandma Lewis brought her oatmeal.

"Don't do it," she said, looking at the packed suitcase that she found hidden under the bed. "You have your whole life ahead of you." Sighing and taking the baby, she added, "You're still a child yourself, Noelle."

Noelle didn't feel like arguing, nor did she feel like a child. Her legs ached, and she was tired. "What are you going to do with her?" she asked her grandmother.

"It's for the best," she said. "She'll be safe and happy and well fed. That's all you can ask for."

"Is it?" she asked.

"That, and some common sense. What were you and that pothead boy thinking?"

/ / /

"GUESS WHO WANTS to see you in her office?" Ron Ingram says over the telephone. "Immediately," he adds.

But he won't go to Stephanie's office. Christopher won't go to work and he'll try not to think about what she is going to tell him. He'll ride the subway and work it out—up to Finch and back down to Bloor, across to Islington and back over to Kennedy—he'll crisscross the city all day if he needs to. Then he will go back to the escalators and maybe one will be going up, and one going down, the way they should be. It will be a normal day, an orange sweater day for sure—it has to be, or he'll never work this out. He will climb away from all the memory he keeps falling into—some place high, somewhere above the lingering fog.

He goes to Broadview station and walks up the street and crosses onto the Bloor-Danforth bridge. There is calm in the valley and bees and bears and honey down there for sure. There is the buzz of traffic on the DVP, and the buzz from smoking half a joint as he walked. The hum of golden bees, round, with sacs of honey strapped to their legs, and the buzz of calmness and his imaginary flight out over the traffic—

above the highway and through the part it makes in the trees, along the winding path, through a wide green door where he imagines a girl sitting in the tall grass, cradling a baby.

Sorry, Christmas Girl. Sorry.

When reality sets in like a concrete block of to-do work tasks, Christopher walks through the Eaton Centre. One escalator going up, the other going down. He takes the escalator under the Michael Snow geese to the second floor and waits on a bench.

/ / /

NOELLE WAITED AT the L'Auberge St. Laurent, and he didn't show. She waited some more and watched the clock and French television. On December 25, baby in her arms, she walked the thousand wooden steps up the side of the snowy mountain, and looked out over Montreal. Then she walked down the same wooden steps, being careful of the ice, and went to Dépanneur Black Cat and spent her last two dollars on a box of powdered milk. She walked with her daughter, who was quiet, her blue eyes open, to a pay phone. She called Wolfville, collect, and her grandmother sent her money for the train.

She moved on to Plan B. She didn't call Christopher when she got to Toronto. She didn't go back to her parents' or finish high school. She worked and studied. She worked as a waitress. She worked as an office temp. She read everything she could get her hands on. She worked in a dry cleaners and she worked in a bookstore. The years passed and she worked at Loblaws as a cashier, and at Business Depot shelving inventory in a warehouse. She wasn't doing bad, but she wasn't doing great either.

She found a job stuffing futons on Bathurst Street. At first the work at Soaring Heart just about killed her. She was exhausted, but then her arms became stronger and so did her back. She learned how to use her legs to hold the case in place as she layered the cotton. She began to like the whole process and to take pride in the work. Each handmade mattress had a signature; customers began to ask for her by name. That's where she met Siovhon. Siovhon was getting her licence to drive a bus.

"That sounds pretty boring," Noelle told her, reaching deep into a half-stuffed case with a fistful of cotton.

"Have you ever driven one?" Siovhon asked.

/ / /

THERE WAS AN enormous oak on a cliff in Bluffer's Park. It was close enough to the edge that she could count the sailboats out on the lake. She sat with her back against the tree—Christopher was asleep with his head in her lap, blond hair curly with sun and sweat. The bark was pressing into her back, but she would not move, could not break from the moment.

They had used her sweater as a blanket. His hand was down her bra, she could hardly breathe. With his fingers inside her she screamed out.

"Shh. Shh, Christmas Girl," he said.

"I can't do this," she said, as he tugged at her jeans.

"I love you," he said, fumbling with her bra, kissing the front of her neck.

In his voice Noelle heard sincerity; against her thigh she felt something that terrified her. But she didn't stop him. Instead, she raised her hips to meet his, moaned inside his mouth.

"Just a little," he said.

/ / /

AT THE INTERVIEW, Noelle was told she had to have her high school diploma and some accident-free driving experience.

No problem.

She was told it was hard work and involved the night shift and some weekends. No problem.

When she went back two years later, she was told they wanted her to start training as soon as possible. They liked her spirit, thought she would be a great driver and good with people.

Noelle walked from the TTC headquarters on Davisville to the St. Clair subway station. She could have flown she was so happy. She ran down the stairway and sat on a bench next to the southbound track. Who would have thought she could drive a bus? Who would have thought she had the nerve to navigate a vehicle the size of Noah's Ark through the jam-packed streets of Toronto?

The southbound train pulled into the station and people hurried off—streams and streams of passengers. Soon it would be her job to get them where they were going. On and off her bus—rough teenagers and wannabe girl and boy models; the rich with broken-down cars, and the poor without a pot to piss in; fresh-out-of-the-shower people with cellphone or coffee in hand; solitary children and grumpy men—all on her filled-to-capacity bus. Noelle stood and walked onto the train. The pull and push as it left the station ran like strong vibrations up and down her legs.

She got out at Queen and took the escalator up to the second floor of the Eaton Centre—above her, the life-sized flock of Canada Geese—always about to land, but never quite touching the ground.

/ MISTER MOOSE EXPERT /

"So . . . Mister Moose Expert," she said, "what else do you know about those head-heavy, butt-ugly creatures?"

We were having lunch at the Arowhon Pines Resort on Little Joe Lake in Algonquin Park. We had been canoeing all morning and decided to stop for a feast before heading into the park for four days of freeze-dried eggs, tofu pasta, and just-add-water chili. Jane's question came after I told her that the moose in the photograph behind our table was young, perhaps two years old.

"Well, the one we saw in the marsh yesterday was very old, probably eight or nine," I said.

Jane always looked great after a few days of fresh air and exercise. Her eyes were lighter, more blue than the fed-up-with-work grey they'd become in recent months. She took off her glasses, crossed her suntanned arms. "Go on," she said.

"I know that he was old because of the size of his antlers and by the way he moved slowly and didn't hide from our canoe."

"Say more," she said, ripping off a chunk of bread and throwing the remaining half of the baguette into the basket between us.

So I did. I told her everything I knew about moose. How they are the largest members of the deer family and their antlers can spread six feet from end to end. How they like to eat tall grasses because it hurts their head to eat close to the ground.

"Yes," I said, reading her grin. "Animals get headaches too. Bad ones."

"Go on," she said, lifting the bowl to her mouth and sipping her soup.

Jane seemed particularly sensitive. More and more, our age difference seems to bother her. It's something I don't give too much thought to until someone reminds me. "Eight years younger than her," they say. "If it was the other way around, and the woman was the younger one, it would be okay." Then they catch themselves. "And this is okay too," they say.

I told her that the bulls are usually very quiet, but it was mating season and they needed to find a mate, so we would likely hear moose calls from our tent at night. I told her that once they do "it," they don't see each other for a year, and even then, they're kind of aloof.

"And, Mister Moose Expert," she asked, the tone of her voice taking a sharp turn, "what kind of a family is that?"

I stood and walked around to her side of the table. It was our tenth anniversary, and her fortieth birthday was less than a week away.

"One that works," I answered, kissing her on the lips. "Moose are passionate and loving creatures."

/ / /

THE LOBBY OF the Algonquin was hectic and everyone seemed busy with someone else. There was no one at the front desk and the service in the Round Table Room was slow. But the fireplace, the lamps with pink shades, the wingback chairs, and the oriental carpets gave the place a calm feel. From where we were sitting, I could see the famous painting of the Vicious Circle. My head was beginning to hurt, and everything was a little blurred, but I didn't need to see the details to know it was her—the exaggerated gestures, the trademark hat and fur coat—Dorothy Parker was the Queen of the Circle. It had been more than twenty minutes since we'd ordered juice and coffee and the waiter was nowhere near our table.

"Let's skip the champagne part," Jane had insisted. "It's too expensive here."

"I can cover it," I smiled. It had been a long time since I'd been able to use that phrase.

"That's okay," she said. "I just don't feel like alcohol."

The waiter was fixated on a table of three girls in their late teens. I could see them laughing and him sucking in his gut, gesturing with his storytelling hand while balancing his enormous tray of drinks with the other.

"I bet our drinks are on that tray," Jane said. "I should just walk over and take them."

"Yeah, right," I said, "*as if.*"

She folded the crossword section of her paper in four, pulled a pencil out of her purse. "You're on thin ice, Mister," she said, pressing her pencil into the page.

"WE COULD GO to the *New Yorker* Festival and stay at the Gonk, drink morning glories in the Round Table Room," I'd said.

"The Gonk?" she'd asked.

"Yeah, the Algonquin. That's what Dorothy Parker used to call it for short."

"Okay. Okay. I get it," she'd said. "I've just never heard it referred to as 'the Gonk.' "

"It will be our tenth anniversary, and we met in Algonquin Park, and it will be your birthday. The Algonquin will be perfect!"

"We could do both," she'd said. "Go camping and then go to New York for the festival after."

"From the ridiculous to the sublime," I'd said.

She had wanted to go to the *New Yorker* Festival for years, but I couldn't afford the trip. We had a deal—if we both couldn't afford to do something, we didn't do it. My income was less than half of hers, so there were lots of things we couldn't afford. Getting the money from John's estate changed a lot. *Be happy* he wrote. *Believe in yourself.* He was the guy I was with when I met Jane. He too was a poet. Sometimes he would come into the store three or four times in one week. One day, he was asking for books on camping.

"You should know by now, John," I said. "We're not so big on camping in this store."

With a stock of mostly fiction, theory, and poetry, This Ain't the Rosedale Library was one of the best literary bookstores in Toronto. John said that he was off on a one-man nature adventure and had no idea where to begin. I recommended Mountain Equipment Co-op and a few other places that could get him moving in the right direction.

"Now, if it were poetry books you were looking for," I said, "I could help."

"What makes you think I'm into poetry?" he said, winking at me.

"Oh, I don't know," I said, laughing. "I was just being random." But of course I wasn't being random. He knew the poetry section better than any of our customers.

"That's the whole point of the canoe trip," he said. "I'm sure the muse is hiding on one of those islands in Algonquin Park." Stuffing the new book into his bag, John added, "She sure isn't hanging out in Kensington."

"I've camped there before," I blurted out just as he got to the door. "It's not a big deal."

"You're into camping?" he asked.

"Well," I said, "not really. But I do know a few things."

"Come with me," he said. "We'll have a blast. We could bring some wine, share the muse . . ."

"I'm not gay, John." I said. I could feel my face burning.

"You're blushing," he said, standing close to me. "I know you're not gay. But I'm very accepting just the same."

/ / /

LATER, IF JANE and I bumped into him at a movie or in a store, we would chat, hug awkwardly. "Let it go," I'd say to Jane.

"Yeah, right," she said. "He's totally in love with you."

"And that curvy little brunette is totally in love with your dick," John said, the day I told him that Jane and I were moving in together. Then he apologized and laughed. "That's kind of funny," he said. "Dick. How's your poetry?

I had no idea that he took my writing seriously. I had no idea he would die of H1N1 at such a young age. Apparently, his immune system had already been jeopardized before the virus came along. I had no idea that he had more than $300,000 invested in a condo that he'd leave me in his will.

/ / /

IT COULD HAVE been my headache, the fact that I had not been able to write a thing the entire trip, or maybe it was waiting so long for our juice from the evasive waiter, but things were not looking good for me and Jane on our last morning in New York. She'd just come back from the washroom, wiping her mouth with Kleenex. She dropped her crutches, plopped back into the chair.

"Did you just throw up?" I asked.

/ / /

I'D THOUGHT THAT a tree had fallen on us. The thud was so intense, the force so fast and heavy. It had landed on the tent just as the sun was coming up. Squinting in the dark, I could see the pink line of the horizon through the tent.

"What the . . . ?" Jane moaned.

"It must be a tree," I said, but my gut told me otherwise. Whatever had fallen on us seemed to be rolling from side to side.

"Are you okay?" I asked, fighting with the zipper. The stupid zipper that always got stuck. Eventually it came loose and I got the flap open.

I could hear Jane struggling to pull herself out from under the weight of whatever had fallen on us. She sounded more frightened than hurt. "Shit," she said. "What the . . . ?"

The cold air hit me, and I was immediately alert—in the dark, the bear looked like a massive black boulder.

"Get out here!" I yelled. "Fast!"

Jane squeezed through the half unzipped door, sprinting into the dark. "Run!" she yelled. "Fast."

There was no time to discuss a plan or draw a map. Intuitively, we both headed in the same direction. Naked, we ran toward the lake. Jane was limping a little, and the bear seemed to be catching up—I couldn't see it, but could feel the thud, hear the growl. Only it was more than a growl, it was the sound a starving animal makes. This was survival. I was sure that one of us was about to die.

"Jump!" she said, taking my hand. I hesitated for only a second. And a second was all that it took for the bear to claw a deep line down Jane's back.

I could hear her yell, but felt the splash of her beside me. *Thank God*, I remember thinking. Thank God.

We could see the bear pacing back and forth above us on the cliff. And, at first, we were just happy to be alive.

"So, Mister Bear Expert," she said, teeth chattering, "you didn't bring food into the tent last night did you?"

/ / /

JANE PRETENDED THAT it was okay that I worked in a bookstore and had aspirations of being an author. She worked for the Ontario Arts Council and earned a decent salary with benefits.

"You know you'll never make a cent off poetry," she said. It was our first night together. "I used to think I wanted to be a writer too," she said. "In high school."

We'd met the day John and I arrived on the island. Jane had already set up camp with her friend Alyssa.

"We have this spot," I attempted to assert myself. It was day five of our trip and I was exhausted.

"Yeah," John said, panting, trying to pull the canoe onto shore by himself. The winds were getting strong and the water was rough.

"Sorry, guys," Jane said, waving a registration form in my face, "it's ours."

"We have one of those too," I said, digging around in my backpack. "Give me a minute."

But we didn't have a minute. It was starting to rain hard.

"We can share," she said, rushing around the campsite, picking things up that were getting wet. "My name is Jane," she said, unzipping the flap of her tent. "Yours?"

/ / /

"IT WAS STUPID," I said. "I've told you ten times it was stupid. Now let it go."

"We could have been killed," she said. "It's not the smartest thing you've ever done."

"Yes. And you've told me that *ad nauseam*."

"Well, come on," she said, shaking her arms at the ceiling fan. "Pepper?"

"Pepper spray," I said. "I'd heard that pepper spray was good against bears. I was told that they hated it, and it seemed to work for me and John those five days."

"In their face!" she yelled. "Not sprinkled over the tent for Pete's sake! You and your little tent buddy just got lucky," she said.

"And what about our fifth anniversary," she went on, "when you read a book on mushrooms and decided to make me a 'special' dinner that got me stoned out of my tree and vomiting for fifteen hours non-stop."

"That wasn't so clever," I said.

"Or the time you were Mister Home Electrician and used lamp wire to fix the sockets in my study?"

"Hmmm," I said. "That did cause a few sparks and a visit from the fire department."

Jane had a sprained ankle and deep scratches on her back from the bear. We both had hypothermia but were released from the hospital in time to go to New York.

"Maybe we shouldn't go camping next year," I said. "I don't know what I would have done if that bear had got you."

"We can still go next year, Mister Bear Protector" she said. "Let's just leave the condiments at home."

"Get over here," I said, pulling her closer to me in the bed.

"Ouch," she said. "Watch the back."

/ / /

"WHAT DO YOU mean, 'as if'?" she asked.

"You've never done anything outside-the-box in your entire life," I said.

"Of course I have," she said.

"Like what?" I asked, but I could tell by the way she was staring down at her hands that she wouldn't be able to come up with anything. I knew that I was being a jerk, but I wasn't able to stop. "Give me one example," I said, but didn't wait for her. "Did you ever sneak into a movie as a kid? Have you ever jaywalked? Parked illegally? Gone over the speeding limit?

"You make it sound like being bad is good."

"It's not being bad," I said. "It's letting go, doing something completely out of character."

"Out of character? Letting go?" She folded the newspaper one more time and placed it on the table between us. "Say more, Mister Moose Expert."

"And that's another thing," I said. "You never call me by my real name."

"Sure I do," she said, scanning the room. "And where's that dumbass, hairy waiter with our bill?"

"Before Mister Moose Expert, I was Mister Fix It. 'Boy, are you good with your hands,' you said. Before Mister Fix It, I was The Terminator. 'You break up with every girl you've ever dated,' you said. That's when you were all hung up about our age difference," I said, looking at her.

"Well, you were only twenty-two back then. Turning thirty was a big deal for me."

"And turning forty is a big deal for you, and turning fifty will be a big deal too. And before The Terminator, I was Christian. 'Why Christian?' I'd asked you back then. 'You know, the long-suffering-penniless-poet from *Moulin Rouge*,' you said. 'Those Ewan McGregor eyes. That kissable mouth.' You don't hear me making fun of your creative aspirations or making up names for you," I said.

"Oh?" she said. "And if you did?"

I took the bait. I headed straight into forbidden territory. "Well," I said. "You could be the Google Goddess, or," I said, looking down at the folded paper, "Queen of Crosswords."

"Go on," she said. "I'm sure there's more."

"Mistress of Culture, Cougar Woman, Sarah Palin . . ."

The last two seemed to hurt most. Folding her arms, she looked away. "Where is that child-chasing waiter?" she said.

"That's it," I said. "You're pissed because he's flirting with those girls and not you."

"I'm pissed because I want to get out of this place," she lied. But the first tear was already there. "Turning forty sucks."

"I'll go get the waiter," I said.

"No," she said. "Mister Avoidance, you're staying put."

"Who?" I asked.

"Mister Avoidance."

"See," I said. "Why won't you call me by my name?"

"It's stupid."

"My name's stupid?"

"I mean who names their kid after a body part?"

"I'm not named after an appendage," I said. "I was named after my dad."

"It just feels weird calling you by the *D* word in public."

"The *D*-word?" I said. "You make a living by assessing funding grants, searching for literary merit in smut and bad erotica, and you can't say 'Dick' out loud?"

"Well, it's not just your name," she said. "It's the combo of your name with mine and the whole plain Jane thing."

"We've talked about this before," I said. "You are anything but plain."

"Sarah Palin?" she said. "That woman's a fascist and a grandmother, for crying out loud!"

"The glasses. The brown hair. There is a resemblance," I said. "Besides, her kid is a teenage mom. Sarah Palin is anything but plain. And, she may be a doorknob, but she's actually kind of hot in a Bible-thumping, crazed-Republican kind of way."

"That's disgusting," she laughed. "Palin aside," she said, putting her hand on her tiny belly. "Don't you think the two of us together is kind of a joke?"

"We're not a joke, Jane," I said.

She picked up the newspaper off the table and turned it over. She held the pencil in her hand, paused just above a blank square "Why do you think I've wanted, for so many years, to get to the festival?" she asked.

"I don't know," I answered. But I did. I saw her writing in her journal every night before bed. I understood why she asked me what books came into the store and which new authors were pushing the envelope. I figured out a long time ago that she too had literary aspirations.

"I grew up with those kids books," she went on, throwing her pencil across the room in the direction of the waiter, who was now standing at the bar with some new twenty-year-old.

"Kids books?" I asked. "What are you talking about?"

"I grew up reading your name with mine, over and over. But I loved those books and wanted to draw my own pictures and write words to go with them."

I could hear that the edge in her voice was gone. Her face was pinker, and her eyes bright with mischief. She motioned for me to sit beside her.

"I'm pregnant," she said.

She'd never talked about kids. Except for the occasional joke about her 'biological clock,' Jane had never once mentioned starting a family in the ten years we'd been together

"I know," I said. "Do you think I'm stupid?"

She turned my face to hers.

"You're taking a little too long to answer that question," I said.

Her hand on my chin was warm. "I'm serious."

"I know you are," I said. "I've listened to you puking every morning for a month now, and I've missed those little white bullets sitting on the back of the toilet."

She was searching the room and smiling. "Is everything okay with us?" she asked, squeezing my hand.

I took her hand and kissed it. "This kid's going to have the most gorgeous mom on the planet," I said. "And stop worrying about the bill," I said. "The waiter gets here when he gets here. How often does Mister Moose Expert find out he's going to be a dad."

But she wasn't listening, she was scanning the room.

"Screw him," she said, shoving her crossword puzzle into her backpack, struggling to get up because of the foot cast.

"Jane . . . ?" I asked. "What are you doing?"

She didn't answer. Balancing herself on one crutch, she started giggling.

"Come on," she said. "You wanted to see 'outside-the-box.'"

"What?" I asked, but she was working her way toward the exit, pushing past the luggage cart and the concierge, laughing and hopping.

I was right behind her, trying not to look back at the growly waiter who finally seemed to notice us. We shoved past the doorman, pushed our way into the flow and chaos of 53rd Street.

"Run, Dick!" she said. "Run, Dick. Run!" she shouted to all of New York.

"WHY WOULD YOU lie about John?" she asked.

Almost two weeks had passed since New York, and things weren't much better. I could feel my throat tighten. *Don't look worried*, I thought to myself. *Act calm.*

"Jane," I said, "where the hell is this coming from?"

"You're not there when we make love. You close your eyes. You're thinking of someone else."

I threw back the covers. "One time, Jane," I said. "One time in ten years I can't get it up and you think I'm gay?"

"You haven't answered my question," she said.

"Why would you care about that now? First of all," I said, sitting on the side of the bed, "I hung out with John for five days, ten years ago. And second," I added, walking around to her side of the bed, "he's dead!" I shouted. "He's dead."

The tears surprised me, as much as they must have surprised her. Not a subtle trickle or gradual flush—I sobbed uncontrollably. Completely let loose. When I finally lifted my head, I looked over to her propped up with pillows in the bed. She hadn't moved. Her face said it all.

"I've never fooled around on you, Jane. John and I had those few days together before we met you on that camping trip, and that's it," I said. "Besides, sexuality is fluid. None of us are plain old gay or straight."

"Well, Mister Sex Expert," she said. "I guess you would know."

"It's like a scale. Most people are more het than queer," I

said. "But some of us straddle the gay-straight scale."

"Scale?" she asked.

"Yes," I said. "On a scale of one hundred, I'm probably seventy percent straight. Most people are around eighty or ninety."

"Well," she said, sitting up in the bed, "your theory sucks. I can think of all kinds of men and women who are a hundred percent straight," she said. "Including me. I've never had a single fantasy of being with another woman."

"It was only five days," I said.

"And he left you his entire estate?"

"It wasn't millions, Jane. It was his condo. That's it."

"But you still think about him," she said. "Don't you?"

For a split second, I thought of lying. "Yes," I said. "I still think about him."

Jane went to the closet and pulled a pair of jeans off a hanger. She put on a sweater and was searching under the bed for her shoes. I watched her for a while, thought about how it was my duty to stay with her, let her have her moment of being pissed. I stood up. It was my duty, but I wasn't going to stay. I pulled on my jeans and went to the bathroom. I brushed my teeth and combed my hair.

"You look gorgeous," she shouted from the bedroom. "Fucking gorgeous."

I put on deodorant and went back into the bedroom.

"Let's talk, Jane," I said, but I didn't mean it.

"Just go," she said. "The Terminator strikes again."

"Now that's just stupid," I said. "Ten years with someone is a pretty good track record."

"Ten years only counts as ten years if you're really there," she said.

/ / /

I'D TOLD HER that moose hooves are just like snowshoes and that's how they get through winter and that baby moose can outrun a human five days after they're born. I said that moose often live alone, and they try to avoid humans whenever possible.

/ / /

THE MOONBEAM IS a carry-over from the early days of Kensington. There aren't too many cafés anymore that haven't been glitzed-up with matching chairs and designer lamps and tables. There aren't too many places where you can hang out for hours with your poetry book and mostly empty journal. I fished around in my backpack for a pen and thought for a moment about Jane's crosswords. My decision to give her the money from the sale of the condo wasn't something I needed to give too much thought to. But, what words? *What words for Jane?* I wondered. I folded the certified cheque and put it in the envelope. I looked at the matching stationary with the bull moose watermark that I had bought in Chinatown—he was a goofy moose with a fat, droopy nose and an overhanging top lip. I pressed the pen into the hump of his shoulders: *Be happy,* I wrote. *Believe in yourself. xoxo Mister Moose Expert.*

/ ACKNOWLEDGEMENTS /

WITH GRATITUDE TO Halli Villegas, Shirarose Wilensky, and the extraordinary team at Tightrope Books.

As always, special thanks to my soulmates at the Phoebe-Walmer Collective for their friendship and love of literature, and to Marnie Woodrow for her compassion and brilliant insights.

"The Singing Driver" was a finalist for the CBC Literary Award and was published in *The White Wall Review*, Issue #34.

"The Girl on the Escalator" was published in *The Puritan*, Issue #6.

"Triptych Twister" was published in *Pilot*, #8.

/ ABOUT THE AUTHOR /

JIM NASON GRADUATED from McGill University with an MA in English Literature. He also holds degrees from Ryerson and York Universities. His award-winning poems, essays, and stories have been published in literary journals and anthologies across the United States and Canada, including *The Best Canadian Poetry in English 2008 & 2010.* He has published two books of poetry: *If Lips Were as Red* (Palmerston Press) and *The Fist of Remembering* (Wolsak and Wynn); a third collection, *Narcissus Unfolding,* is forthcoming from Frontenac House. His debut novel, *The Housekeeping Journals,* was released to critical acclaim by Turnstone Press in 2007. He has been a finalist for the CBC Literary Award in both the fiction and poetry categories. He lives in Toronto.